In this new volume, Josh Moody provides careful, thoughtful, and insightful responses in a readable and accessible manner to the some of the most difficult and challenging issues related to the nature, authority, and interpretation of the Bible. Engaging ten of the most common questions related to the Bible in a warm, pastoral, and practical manner, Moody not only points the way for his readers but offers an encouraging and exemplary guide for pastors, teachers, and theologians who also wish to communicate important truths in an effective and understandable way. I highly recommend *How the Bible Can Change Your Life* and trust that it will receive a wide readership.

David S. Dockery
PRESIDENT, TRINITY INTERNATIONAL UNIVERSITY

I'm a huge fan of books on the doctrine of Scripture. Get the Bible right, and everything falls into place. Get the Bible wrong, and everything falls apart. Josh Moody's latest book certainly helps you do the former! Both apologetic and devotional, full of theory and of practice, reading *How the Bible Can Change Your Life* has the feel of a relaxed chat over coffee with an extremely knowledgeable friend who wants you to help you grow. And who's convinced that the means to such growth is 'every word that comes from the mouth of God.' Read it, and then let the Bible change your life.

Dave Gobbett
LEAD PASTOR, HIGHFIELDS CHURCH, CARDIFF AND WORD ALIVE TRUSTEE

Many today are questioning the authority, relevance, and applicability of the Bible. Despite recent concerted efforts at encouraging Bible engagement, even many Christians seem to be in doubt about the usefulness of Scripture to their lives. Many learned books have been written by top notch scholars on issues relating to the authority, relevance, interpretation and practical applicability of the Bible, but the fruit of their labours have rarely been accessible to ordinary Christians. Josh Moody's book helps bridge the gap between the academy and the ordinary church member. The rare combination of scholar and grassroots minister has resulted in a highly readable book that is nevertheless based on sound scholarship.

Ajith Fernando
TEACHING DIRECTOR, YOUTH FOR CHRIST, SRI LANKA

Every generation needs to meet God through his self-revelation in the Bible, but today prejudices and objections as to why not seem to multiply. In this readable, pithy, up to date approach, Dr Josh Moody delves beneath the bland assumptions to expose the inadequacy of their thinking and answer the objections. A powerful blend of penetrating argument and practical application, this is a God-centred challenge to prevailing contemporary attitudes. It will send you back to the Bible with renewed confidence and fresh expectation. It will get you off the back foot and equip you to present the Bible's message more cogently and unapologetically to our needy, lost generation. Every Christian should read it!

David Jackman
FOUNDER OF CORNHILL TRAINING COURSE, FORMER PRESIDENT OF THE PROCLAMATION TRUST

How the Bible Can Change Your Life may well change your life because the Bible is that life-changing. Josh Moody knows this truth and has staked his life upon it. Moody's book will greatly help a wide range of readers-- the beginner, the Bible-hungry believer, the confused--and will minister particularly to the brilliant thinker who needs strong but succinct arguments dipped in supernatural realities. Moody is just this kind of thinker, and he is thus fearsomely well equipped to teach sound doctrine, exegete tough passages, and handle understandable objections. The great need of the modern church is confidence in and affection for the Word of God. *How the Bible Can Change Your Life* is just the book for times like ours.

Owen Strachan
ASSOCIATE PROFESSOR OF CHRISTIAN THEOLOGY, MIDWESTERN SEMINARY;
CO-AUTHOR OF *THE GRAND DESIGN: MALE AND FEMALE HE MADE THEM*

JOSH MOODY

How the Bible Can Change Your Life

ANSWERS TO THE TEN MOST COMMON
QUESTIONS ABOUT THE BIBLE

TRUTHFORLIFE®
CHRISTIAN
FOCUS

Josh Moody has asserted his right under the Copyright, Designs and Patents Act, 1988, to be identified as Author of this work.

paperback ISBN 978-1-5271-0151-7
epub ISBN 978-1-5271-0220-0
mobi ISBN 978-1-5271-0221-7

First published in 2018

Reprinted in 2019
by
Truth for Life,
P.O. Box 398000
Cleveland, OH 44135
and
Christian Focus Publications Ltd,
Geanies House, Fearn, Ross-shire
IV20 1TW, Scotland, UK
www.christianfocus.com

A CIP catalogue record for this book is available from the British Library.

Designed and typeset by Pete Barnsley (Creativehoot.com)

Printed in the U.S.A.

Contents

Dedication

This one is for Sophia

Introduction

Christians are Bible people. We believe that God speaks to us through the Bible, and that God has inspired – that is, breathed out – the words of the Bible. We believe that the Bible points us to Jesus Christ, and that 'faith comes from hearing, and hearing through the Word of Christ' (Rom. 10:17). We believe that 'All Scripture is breathed out by God and profitable for teaching, for reproof, for correction, and for training in righteousness' (2 Tim. 3:16), and that 'the word of God is living and active, sharper than any two-edged sword, piercing to the division of soul and of spirit, of joints and of marrow, and discerning the thoughts and intentions of the heart' (Heb. 4:12). We believe that 'the words of the LORD are pure words, like silver refined in a furnace on the ground, purified seven times' (Ps. 12:6).

We believe all this but there is a gap between our profession and our practice. Some Christians rarely read the Bible on their own at all, and those who do have 'devotions' or 'quiet times' will give more attention to the inspiring commentary on the Bible rather than to the inspired word of the Bible.[1] Some churches, I am very much afraid, give little attention to the Bible as well, and so it is not surprising that Christians follow the practice of their leaders as they shape their worship services without time for the teaching of the Bible. These days you can go to church services and find

---

1   This issue is explored more in chapter 7.

the Bible remains studiously unopened altogether, let alone see any finer points of the right way to do exposition.

The reason for this gap between our profession and our practice is twofold.

On the one hand, we live with the fruit of what is now centuries of academic disillusionment with the historical reliability and the authority of the Bible. This doubt of, if not attack on, the Bible, has over time inevitably filtered down first to the mainline or liberal churches, and then gradually even to those that are evangelical. When you can find innumerable, learned-sounding critiques exposing the so-called faults of the Bible, on YouTube or various blogs, it begins to cut well-meaning Christian confidence at the knees.

The other reason for this gap, though, is a little more recent. The argument is being made, and increasingly heeded, that to use the Bible in church – and thereafter in Christian witness and perhaps in Christian devotion – is not only unnecessary but unhelpful. Because, it is said, we live in a post-literate age, we must all adjust, and talk about what God says in the Bible. but not actually explain the Bible itself. The trouble with this argument is, of course, that while we may or may not live in a post-literate age, we are certainly not the first age that was non-literate. The Bible was itself written at a time when most people actually could not read or write at all—rather than simply did not choose to do so. You could argue, in fact, that more is being read today than ever before; it is just that it is being read in electronic in addition to print form.

At any rate, for the sake of this book, I am going to take it for granted that both tendencies are unwelcome to my readers. The more pressing issue then is what to do about them? In at least a rather small way I hope the answer is: read and disseminate this book. My goal in writing it is to follow on from the previous book in this series (*How Church Can Change Your Life*) by tackling the next great challenge for contemporary Christians: faith in and practice of the Bible itself. I have taken the same approach to the structure of the book. Relying on thousands of conversations with many people over the years, I have constructed what I take to be the 'ten most common questions' that people tend to ask about Scripture. The goal is to bridge that gap between our profession and our practice with regard to the Bible. And to show therefore that the Bible can and does change our lives.

My ultimate goal, as always, is for the glory of God. *Soli Deo Gloria.*

Is the Bible True?

If you're a Christian, then you know that you are meant to assume that the Bible is true, but you may secretly wonder whether it is actually all that it is cracked up to be. If you're not a Christian, or not sure whether you are, then you probably think that the claim that the Bible is true, in any literal or factual sense, is borderline laughable—even if you're too polite to come right out and say as much to your Christian friends.

The reality is that since the Enlightenment, the fulcrum of modern science and rationalism in the eighteenth century there have been many scholarly criticisms of the Bible.

But what is new in the last, say, twenty years or so, is that these well-worn (to academics) criticisms of the Bible have been gradually making their way more and more into the popular realm. Part of this is that, because of the Internet, information is far more widely available than ever before. Part of it is because a group sometimes dubbed 'neo-atheists' have decided that the best way to prevent religious extremism from taking hold is to attack the

1

certainties that Christians have traditionally had about the Bible (though you wonder sometimes why they don't expend as much energy utilizing the orientalists' historical criticisms of the Koran). But whatever the reason, more people than ever today are aware that there is – and has been for a long time – a group of sophisticated academics who lampoon the idea that the Bible is in any sense 'true.'

This apparently puts Christians on the back foot, having to defend the Bible and answer the questions being asked of it. We will answer some of those questions, though inevitably in a somewhat brief and non-technical way, in this book and in particular in this chapter. But it is important, first of all, to get back on the front foot and take the initiative against the historical criticisms of the Bible at their source, the very fount of such criticisms.

At root, these criticisms are making a number of untested and unwarranted assumptions. Above all, they are assuming that the miraculous does not happen. Now, we who are Christians need to be careful not to give the impression that we think that miracles happen all the time. On the contrary, by definition miracles are rare events; otherwise, they would be called 'normal life,' not miracles.

But, by the same token, there is an untested assumption at the back of much criticism of the Bible which is that prophecies, turning water into wine, and the like, *cannot* happen, therefore *did not* happen, and so there must be a different explanation to the miracles as recorded.

I recall one school teacher of mine when I was young explaining away the fall of the walls of Jericho along these lines.

According to him – because it was simply impossible to believe that God made the walls fall down – what really happened was as follows.

The people inside the walls became more and more terrified watching the Israelites march around. And then when, on the last day, the Israelites shouted and blew their trumpets, fear overwhelmed the city and they all threw open the doors to the city. The description of the 'walls falling down' was an ancient way of saying that they 'opened the gates'. I remember, even then, thinking, *Well, if you can believe that, you can believe anything! So … someone is terrified by a surrounding army—and their response is to open all the doors to let the army in? Yeah, right. That would be like someone being terrified of flying and so opening the plane door midflight and jumping out. Right. That makes sense.*

If you assume that the miraculous cannot happen, you are forced to find alternative explanations. Isaiah could not have made predictions about the emperor Cyrus, so—there must have been three Isaiahs. On and on it goes: but the root assumption needs to be brought out into the light and examined on its own merits. You are saying that miracles do not happen. Which means you are really saying that whatever God there may be is not the kind of God who can do miracles. Which means that you are already assuming that the kind of God that the Bible describes does not in any real sense exist. Which means that you are dismissing the Bible's claims to truth based upon a set of presuppositions which may or may not be accurate. Which means that by using those presuppositions you are shielding yourself from the very evidence (the Bible) that might help you question whether your assumptions are indeed correct.

The easiest way to see the astonishing bias that these historical criticisms of the Bible have is in the way that they treat other ancient historical documents quite differently.

It is a fact of surpassing strangeness that at the very same time that the Biblical Studies Departments at elite universities were becoming more cynical about the texts they were studying, right across the street, in the Classics Departments, they were growing more confident about the veracity of the texts that they were studying. And both were employing rational, scientific, modern tools! But, in the one case, there were no miraculous or demanding moral claims being made on their lives. In the other, it challenged the philosophical assumptions and committed lifestyles of the people looking at the texts. Interestingly enough, in some universities, because of these dynamics, more senior professors who take a more conservative approach to the Bible are being appointed to Biblical Studies Departments. The popular Internet is yet to catch up with this trend; wait ten years and it will be more evident!

Leaving biases and prejudices about the miraculous to the side, then: is the Bible true? For it to be true the Bible must be *historically accurate*, *scientifically commensurate*, and *ethically acceptable.*

Historically accurate

The Bible is a historical book. That does not mean that it only talks about past events: the Bible has predictions about the future – 'a new heaven and a new earth' (Isa. 65:17; Rev. 21:1) – and it is readily applicable to everyday events today. Christians believe that it is 'living and active' (Heb. 4:12), and that when they read the Bible, it speaks to them right now. Nonetheless, however, the Bible was written in the past: its claims to be true are made within the truth-claims of historicity.

There are other kinds of truth claims beside those of historical truth. Empirical science, what used to be called 'natural philosophy', makes its claim to truth based upon a mix of Karl Popper's famous 'potentially falsifiable' standard for scientific truth claims, and the empirical method of observation, hypothesis, testing, and then establishing a theory which makes best sense of available data.

If you approach the Bible's truth claims assuming it is testable in an empirical, scientific sense, you will rapidly become deeply frustrated. You cannot test the Bible in that sense; you cannot put the truth claims of the Bible in a laboratory and perform natural scientific tests to verify its truth claims. That does not mean that its truth is not even, as Karl Popper would say, 'potentially falsifiable'; that it does not even raise to the level of being a real truth claim at all. For there are other kinds of truth claims beside the scientific, empirical method that Popper was describing. Some of these truth claims are mainly subjective, or a matter of personal opinion—as in the 'truth' that a certain piece of art is better than another piece of art; 'beauty is in the eye of the beholder.'

There are methods, in fact, at arriving at *objective* truth in addition to, and supplemental to, empirical testing. For instance:

The truth claims of philosophy. Some of that may seem like going round and round in circles to you, but the principles and reasoning are well established within the history of philosophy.

The truth claims of a court of law. Legal truth may not reach the level of ultimate truth. But the law, when due process is followed, is recognized the world over as eventually being able to arrive at the closest thing we can discover in this world to the truth about an event or a dispute.

The truth claims of economics. For sure, economics (sometimes rather unfairly called 'the dismal science') struggles to make certain predictions. But there are basic economic rules and principles which, irrespective of which competing school of economics you belong to, are recognized as being true.

The truth claims of history. If we could find nothing to be true from history, we would have little certain truth. All our knowledge, information, and truth-gathering in society relies upon our ability to learn and record the recognizable truth of history, from recent years to the distant past.

That all other truth claims are somehow less objective than those of natural science is simply not the case The reality is that truth claims of natural science change over the years; what was received wisdom yesterday may be outmoded trash tomorrow. There are 'paradigm shifts' (in Thomas Kuhn's phrase) that take place within the scientific guild as much as anywhere else.

It is important to emphasize that the Bible was written in the past, and that therefore its truth claims are historical claims, so that we can then make sure we assess those truth claims by the right methods.

Historical facts are established by a simple methodology.

First of all, there must be some record. That record could be oral history (the passing of the truth from mouth to ear, recorded in human memory, and then retold again), but obviously oral history has a tendency to become distorted over time because of the vagaries of human memory. More commonly, historians base their assessment of facts on some sort of written or physical record. In recent history that could be a video (for instance, of the Vietnam War); in very ancient times it could be an archaeological remain of some clay pot or a 'bulla' (seal). Most commonly, it is a written record.

Second, that written record is then assessed for its veracity and reliability. It is assessed based upon the reliability of the author of that record. If the author is known to be a liar from other evidence, that obviously influences the extent to which you take what they say seriously. If they have a well-known bias to advocate for some event or other, that also influences your assessment of the data. If the author himself saw the event, then that becomes stronger evidence. If instead they rely on other eyewitnesses, but if the author actually interviewed those witnesses, that is different than if their evidence has become distant from the original event by some long gap.

Then, third, having assessed the reliability of the author, the reliability of the record itself must be assessed. Is this the original? Is this a copy of a copy of a copy? Is the copy originating within the lifetime of those who could deny or confirm the truth of what is being said? Are there other corroborating records that document compatible evidence that mutually confirm the truth claim?

If there is a reliable record, if it is written by an author who is known to be reliable, if the copy of the record is written close to the event, and the copy is known to be accurate because of the expertise of the scribes, then for all intents and purposes, what we are dealing with is a truth claim that is true—in the same way that empirical science establishes a theory that is the best working paradigm for the available data.

There is another level of 'interpretation' to mention, which is where most of the work of professional historians goes; here motives, rationales, and causes are debated and discussed. These are by nature more subjective. For instance, no one doubts that King Henry VIII had six wives. This is a historical fact. But exactly why he had six wives, what motivated him to divorce one and behead another, what sort of person Henry was to treat his wives this way, how much he was motivated by politics or religion—all this is endlessly debated. But no one doubts the fact that he had six wives! It is important to make this distinction because a lot of professional theologians utilize the evidence and work of professional historians without understanding the difference between these two kinds of history; you cannot rely absolutely as a truth claim upon one particular view about why Henry did something – or why Paul did something – but you can rely upon the fact that Henry existed and that Paul existed.

So, then, based upon this methodology of historical truth claims, leaving as unvoiced for the moment the power of God to witness to His own Word through what theologians call 'illumination' and the work of the Spirit, are the claims of the Bible true?

Obviously, this is a huge subject, not just because of all the books and conversation about it over the years, but also because the Bible itself was written over a very long period of time by different human authors. It is quite impossible to exhaustively answer that question in this chapter of this book—or any one human book or conversation, for that matter.

But what we can say is the following.

Don't prejudge the Bible

If you found a legal document that described magical fairies in the courtroom, you would doubt the validity of that legal record as a whole. But the presence of miracles recorded in the Bible cannot by itself be used to dismiss the rest of the Bible, any more than if a time traveler came to our present time and saw mobile phones in use, they would be right to dismiss the mobile Internet as impossible before they considered the evidence. You should not prejudge by intellectual bias before assessing the evidence. As Sherlock Holmes said: When all the other options have been ruled out, what is left, however strange, must be the truth. Do not assume that Jesus' resurrection from the dead *could not* have happened. If all other ways of explaining the beginning of the church are ruled out logically – as I think they are – then you are faced with a truth claim about the resurrection of Jesus physically from the dead which is true. Astonishingly, beautifully, true.

Start with Jesus

We know as a historical fact that Jesus existed. This is certain not just because of His huge influence on history subsequently, not only and most importantly because of the record of the New Testament, but also because of the records of non-Christian authors about Jesus (for instance Josephus, Tacitus, and Suetonius).

Now let us consider what the New Testament, and in particular Luke's gospel, says about Jesus. Luke's gospel is a verifiably reliable, historical document. It was written by a person close to the events. It was written based upon eyewitness accounts. Its data is corroborated by what else we know about the ancient world at the time. Luke has no reason to lie about who Jesus is; in fact, he has the strongest possible reason to either pretend that Jesus does not exist or deny His divinity: persecution was coming soon. Who would die for a lie?

So let us read Luke's gospel and ask ourselves, who is this Jesus that is being described here? When we read about Jesus, we find that we encounter a person who claims to be the Lord, the Son of God, the Messiah. We can deny that claim and say that He was lying; we can deny that claim and say that He was insane. But we, as C.S. Lewis famously argued in his trilemma, cannot say that He was merely a 'good man'.

Let us say, then, that we become convinced that Jesus is admirably and compellingly the Lord of all. Having spent time studying the New Testament, we come to a point of conviction that Jesus is who He claimed to be: the Son of the Living God, Jesus the Christ.

Now, let us further, therefore, ask ourselves how Jesus treated the Scriptures of the Old Testament and how He commissioned His apostles to carry His message (in person and in writing) based upon their witness of and testimony to Him. We find that He treated the Scriptures as what God said (Matt. 19:4-5; cf. Gen. 2:23) and commissioned His apostles with the authority to remember, recall, speak and so write in His name (John 14:26).

Here is Jesus.

We follow Him.

Here is His approach to Scripture.

If we follow Jesus, we will follow His approach to Scripture.

We therefore accept it as *true*.

Compare other ancient texts

We know as a historical fact that Caesar invaded Britain. We know this based upon his own account of the invasion—a biased and politically motivated account. Caesar's *Gallic Wars* was written somewhere between 58 to 50 B.C. The oldest surviving copy we have of the *Gallic Wars* is from about A.D. 850. That is a time gap of 900 years. And we have in existence a sum total of ten manuscript copies of Caesar's *Gallic Wars*.

Now compare that with the New Testament.

The New Testament was written somewhere between about A.D. 42 and 90. The earliest surviving manuscript of a gospel is something called the Rylands papyrus and is dated at A.D. 125. (There is an earlier copy of a piece of Matthew's gospel in the library of Magdalen College, Oxford, which Carsten Thiede dated controversially to A.D. 52.) So the time lapse between the writing of the document and the earliest manuscript copy is about 35 years. And the number of manuscripts – many of them only partial – that survive? 24,000 or so manuscripts.

So we have a reliable author, Luke, biased if anything to claim that Jesus was *not* Lord (for to claim He *was* Lord was a potential death sentence).

We have corroborative evidence that supplements the manuscripts of the New Testaments and confirms their basic picture of life at the time.

We have a very brief gap between the original and the copy, with many manuscripts of various sizes and types still in existence. Caesar's *Gallic Wars* is a nine-hundred-year gap, ten-copy claim to truth; the gospels are a thirty-five-year gap, tens-of-thousands-of-copies claim to truth.

If you remove presupposition and prejudice that the miraculous cannot happen, then you are left with a strong case that the Bible is indeed true.

Scientifically commensurate

By 'scientifically commensurate' I mean not that what the Bible says is compatible with what we currently think is true based on the latest scientific theory. That could suggest that the authority of the Bible is checked by novel human opinions. I mean that it is 'commensurate': the approach that the Bible takes fits with or matches an approach that is supportive of scientific investigation.

That begs a question: is what we currently think to be true based on the discoveries of modern science really in fact true? We know that science changes its mind from time to time. To take the most celebrated example (and often used to attack the Bible): do we live in a heliocentric or geocentric galaxy? In other words, does the sun go around the Earth or does the Earth go around the sun? The Copernican view, adopted by Galileo, repressed by the Roman Catholic church, was believed by some to be antithetical to various texts in the Bible that talk of the sun rising and setting. But that description of the sun rising and setting was never intended to be what we would call a 'scientific' description. It is a simple description of how things appear to be to a person walking about this planet that we call Earth. If I asked you, 'When is sunset?' you would not thereby assume that I am making a claim that the sun goes around the Earth (rather than the other way around).

The reason why the Roman Catholic church resisted Galileo's more scientifically accurate model of the galaxy was because his viewpoint was gathering traction among the Protestant Reformers at the time. Galileo was viewed as potentially heretical because there were those, from the Reformers' camp, who were leaning towards the Copernican view of the universe. As Galileo himself remarked, 'All the most distinguished heretics [that is the Reformation leaders] accepted Copernican doctrines.' There is evidence that it was in particular the Jesuits, who were formed with the mission to counter and defeat the Reformation, that drove Galileo's heresy trial. Father Grienberger, later leader of the Jesuit College, said, 'If Galileo had not incurred the displeasure of the Company [that is, the Jesuits], he could have gone on writing freely about the motion of the Earth to the end of his days.'[1] The 'Galileo-thing' was more about a debate between Roman Catholics and Protestants than between the Bible and science.

Now we live in an Einstein universe, where his theories of special and general relativity are accepted, and the whole idea of a 'center' to the universe is suspect. It all depends from what part of the universe you are taking your perspective. While it is still more accurate to talk about the Earth going around the sun (than the other way around), the whole debate appears somewhat archaic because it was given heat by a different model of the universe than the one we at the moment hold to be accurate.

But what about the origins debate? Surely, people would say, science has established evolution as the only workable scientific model. Therefore, is it not the case that the description in the Bible of Genesis chapters 1 and 2 is entirely 'non-commensurate' with what we know to be true?

The trouble with answering this aspect of the question is that the right response is hotly debated among Christians. There are some Christians who feel very strongly that evolution, of whatever kind, is antagonistic to the Christian gospel. There are other Christians who are quite happy to at least potentially agree to a science of evolution—though they would still

---

1   Denis Alexander, *Rebuilding the Matrix: Science and Faith in the 21st Century* (Lion, 2001), p. 120.

strongly resist the naturalist philosophy and reductionistic assumptions of atheistic evolution. The important point to grasp is that the Bible itself does not teach that if you accept the science of evolution you cannot believe the Bible. Augustine, writing a long time before Darwin, viewed Genesis chapter 1 in a non-literal way because the text itself indicated as much. If there is light before the sun is created, Augustine thought, then the message of Genesis chapter 1 cannot be taken as a literal text book. It has a bigger and more important meaning than the *engineering* of creation—it is about the *creation* of creation. Not to mention, in addition, that thinking of anything in the Bible as literally scientific is a kind of anachronism. Science, as we know it, did not even begin until about 500 years ago, a long, long time after Genesis chapter 1 was written.

The Bible is not against reason, science and learning. Far from it: there is an assumption throughout the Bible that God's Word gives light to our path. Jesus *is* the Logos or Word. Jesus *is* the light. Christianity is a religion of light (not darkness), of reason and logic (not irrationality), and it has been at the forefront of the birth of science, the universities, the hospitals, modern democracy, and many of the foundational elements of civilized societies.

Ethically acceptable

Not too long ago it would have seemed absurd to doubt the ethically-acceptable nature of the Bible. We took it for granted that the Bible occupied the high moral ground. Those who follow it were those who were at least trying to be moral, sometimes even coming across as claiming to be *more* moral than the rest of us ('holy Joes', Christians have in the past been called disparagingly).

Nowadays, however, people look at the bloodshed in the Bible, particularly in the Old Testament, and wonder whether it is really a moral book after all. Some even look at the cross, with its death and gore, and wonder whether having a symbol at the heart of a person's faith that is so violent could legitimate bloodshed, even be reflected in the violence of the history of Christendom.

Part of the answer to this moral aspect of the question 'Is the Bible true?' will come subsequently (see chapter 9). For now, though, let us turn this charge against the Bible on its head.

Has there ever been a higher statement of moral standards than Jesus' Sermon on the Mount? Who else ever commanded us to 'love your enemies and pray for those who persecute you' (Matt. 5:44)? What is more, do we really want to live in a universe where there is never any final justice? Plainly, evil does occur in this world. Are we saying that we want to live in a universe where that evil never receives its appropriate justice? Do we want the Hitlers of this world never to receive their comeuppance? If we want there to be justice, in what sense can we honestly claim to not also be those who are worthy of being on the wrong end of judgment (certainly when we judge our lives by that Sermon on the Mount, adulterers and murderers at heart as we all are)?

And what greater love is there than this, that someone lays down His life for His friends (John 15:13); that Christ gave His life for us that we might go free? What greater holiness or morality could there be than that 'God demonstrates his own love for us in this: While we were still sinners, Christ died for us' (Rom. 5:8, NIV)?

In short, those who charge that the Bible is unethical have not come to grips with the inner structure and texture of the story of the Bible, understanding how the goodness of God, His holiness, and His love, even towards rebels like us, is met in the sacrificial death of the Son of God.

In all, the best answer to the question about the truth of the Bible is *tolle lege*—as the little child's game said to the great Augustine. 'Take and read' the Bible. Discover its truth for yourself. It is sweeter than honey.

A story

Frank had only heard about the Bible—and what he had heard was not encouraging. Apparently, it was just old mythical stories about people invading other people's countries and ethnically cleansing whole nations. He was rather surprised, then, when he actually read the Bible for himself and started with the Sermon on the Mount. Who is this that tells us to love our enemies and pray for those who persecute us? It made him rethink the whole thing.

Gradually, bit by bit, as he read more and talked about it with friends, he began to find that the Bible was sweeter than honey. It was a strange thing: he had never been much of a reader. But reading the Bible was more like an experience, an encounter, listening to a voice. Somehow it had hands and feet and ran after him; it had a voice that spoke to him. He was hooked, but in a good way. He had found the words of eternal life, and he did not ever want to leave them again.

Questions for discussion

1. Do you think it is possible to be a scientist and also believe in the Bible?

2. Do you think you can have a high view of reason and still also believe in the Bible?

3. How would you answer the question, 'Why do you believe the Bible is true?'

4. What could you do today to start finding out about the truthfulness of the Bible for yourself?

5. What new areas of your life could you submit to the truth claims of the Bible?

QUESTION 2

Is the Bible Relevant?

You might think that if the Bible is true, then it must also be relevant, but that is not necessarily the case. Many people are willing to accept that the Bible has historical truthfulness to it in some sense or other, but still believe what the Bible says is no longer relevant. The thinking goes along these lines: 'That kind of morality was fine for Paul, but we don't live in those old days any more. In ancient times people thought about sex in that kind of way, but nowadays we know that is all nonsense. Before people became scientific, they were willing to accept fanciful or miraculous interpretations of facts, but we know better today.'

The relevance question is a remarkably anthropocentric kind of question to ask of the Bible. It exposes the modern world's human-centered fascination with utility, function, productivity, or relevance, as opposed to the more timeless truths of beauty and glory. Let's look at each of the logical fallacies that nestle behind the relevance question, like shy 1950s schoolgirls blushing behind their pigtails, and then conclude the answer to this question to show the relevance of the Bible even within the terms and definition of the original question.

The assumption of 'chronological snobbery'

The idea that the past is always less advanced than the present could be dubbed 'chronological snobbery,' as C.S. Lewis so memorably called the assumption that what happened in the past is more likely to be wrong than what is happening today. Of course, there is what you might call an 'inverse chronological snobbery' that assumes that the past is always better than the present or the future. Both approaches are understandable to some extent. Many people tend to a view that life was better in the 'good old days' and so by extension could view that the kind of life described in the Bible might be better than life as it is today. On the other hand, it is quite obvious that various aspects of contemporary life are easier than they were not so long ago: airplanes that can fly, cars that drive, basic health and hygiene, and medical advances. None of these advances can be gainsaid even if they have come at some cultural and environmental cost at the same time.

But there is another way of looking at the Bible than simply whether its relevance is determined by your view of whether the past was better or worse than life today. That way is to understand that while the Bible is a historical book, it is also a timeless book. The claim – one that we are examining by means of these various common questions asked about the Bible – then is that the Bible is not only written by humans, but also inspired by God. Obviously, the human element of the Bible can be subject to various time-bound factors of human progress, and moral regression too. But the timeless aspect, the aspect of the Bible that is inspired (as the scholars would say, 'plenary inspiration': fully inspired) by God, cannot be so limited or subject to the relevance question. The question of relevance is based upon a modern view of time: as things move forward, we leave behind old ways of doing things and pick up new ways of doing them. Depending on what you think about that assumption will determine how you approach things (including the Bible) from the past: interesting, relevant, outmoded, or pointless.

But what if the Bible is not merely a historical document but also – as it claims – a living document? What if it is 'living and active' (Heb. 4:12)? It would take a very rude person to walk up to their neighbor, living and actively walking across the street, and say to them that they are not relevant! You might not like your neighbor, you might disagree with them, but you are not going to say they are not relevant.

Similarly, if it is true that the Bible is not simply a historical document, but the living Word of God, speaking today for those with ears to hear, and that reading the Bible is having an active experience of listening to God's voice now—if that is true, then whatever else it may be, it is certainly relevant.

The anthropocentric logical assumption

To be anthropocentric is to settle on looking at life from a human-centered point of view. Of course, if you think that God does not exist, then you are likely to end up with some sort of anthropocentric view of life (unless you take a radical 'Gaia' approach to center upon nature or the universe itself, and people as being just one – perhaps the most advanced entity – among many other living things). The opposite to an anthropocentric view is a theocentric, or God-centered, view of life, and it is this view that is foundational to the way the Bible looks at things. It starts with the presumption of the existence of God, and that God speaks, that He is revealing Himself to us through His

Word. Given that assumption, what the Bible says is relevant—if there is a God, and if He speaks, and if the Bible is where He speaks, then clearly what is being said is relevant, or important, or of consequence to us all. So nestled behind the relevance question is really an anthropocentric, or a humanistic, assumption. If God does not exist, or at least if He is silent and is not revealing Himself, then of course what the Bible says – which is largely about God and what He wants from His creation – is completely irrelevant. It might have fantastical fascination, like a word of fiction or surreal art. It might have value as a work of literature. It may have importance as a cultural factor of what people used to think in the old days. But it is not relevant; it does not have anything of importance to say today.

So the question of relevance is really a code for saying either that the Bible is merely a historical document (and therefore not 'living and active' today), or that God is merely a figment of imagination (and therefore cannot say anything today). Both those claims may be true, but they are nestled behind the relevance question as unguarded assumptions and therefore themselves have to be answered before assuming the relevance question to be true. It's like saying that a brand-new warship has no more relevance for the conditions that we find ourselves in today. Why would that claim be made? Because it is assumed that the battles of the future will be taking place in a certain kind of way that means that the sort of warship that is being built is no longer relevant to those new battles. But if it is found out that actually that assumption is incorrect, that the battles of today and tomorrow are going to be ones in which this new warship does and will play an important role, then obviously it is now very much relevant. Similarly, if the Bible is inspired by God, and if God does exist, then the relevance question is answered because the assumptions on which it is based are answered.

The utility assumption

The final assumption nestled behind the relevance question is not that the Bible is merely a historical document or that God is merely a figment of our human imagination. This final assumption is based upon what makes something relevant at all. It tends towards a utilitarian approach to life. In other words, show me the numbers. It is the strip-mall approach to truth, the shopping mall approach to human flourishing, the concrete block version of aesthetics. In fact, there are no real aesthetics at all. Everything is based upon whether it makes money or increases productivity and therefore has utility. There is no place for the underlying virtues that give rise to productivity (like character), and certainly not any place for there being a higher virtue to things and people than simply whether they are productive and useful. Often the Bible is viewed as irrelevant by busy men and women of the world because they see it as a waste of time. They have places to be and things to do, deals to make and money to exchange, stocks to buy and sell, positions of authority to be candidate for—the idea of sitting down (as Blaise Pascal would say) in a quiet room by themselves for an hour is anathema. And reading the Bible, because it is not a 'how-to' manual for the best way to be rich and famous in as short a time as possible, is viewed as a complete waste of time.

But, again, what an assumption! Could it be that there is something more important than making money, or climbing the slippery pole of career and power? Could it be that our lives are not merely the sum total of our productivity? Could there be something called beauty and something called truth, something called life and something called hope, something called love and something called joy? People who wrestle with these kinds of questions, if they are Christians, tend to turn the Bible into a series of how-to instructions. They will ask what the practical takeaway is of any sermon, Christian book, teaching, or culture. What they are really asking is how this helps them become more useful, more utilitarian, more productive, more able to get more things done in a shorter space of time. But perhaps, could it be, that the Bible actually wants us to be still and know that God is God (Psalm 46:10)? To gaze with unadorned face at the glory of Christ? To experience Jesus—not like experiencing a drug, but like experiencing the relationship that is the source of all loving relationships?

For instance, could it be that a tree is only relevant if it is useful? That it only justifies its existence by producing an efficient cleanup of carbon dioxide and emittance of oxygen? Could it be, instead, that its value is found in what it simply *is*, a fine tree-y version of a real tree?

There is more to life, the Bible assumes, than productivity, and the relevance question has nestled in its set of assumptions a sort of modernistic, industrialized version of value as utilitarianism.

What then of the relevance of the Bible in a more positive sense—and not just defending it from the charge of irrelevance based upon false, modernistic, human-centered assumptions? If only space could allow more articulation and indeed celebration! Simply, though, ask yourself: Do people still die, wrestle with guilt, wonder what is the meaning of life? Do people continue to get married, get into arguments, fall in love, have children, work, play, and worship? I deliberately leave the word 'worship' until last, not because I think it is not actually primary (which it is), but because the Bible answers far more questions than simply, if massively, 'how we are meant to do church'. If you are facing the perennial questions that have faced every human being that ever there was – where do I come from and where am I going and how do I make the most of the time allotted to me – then the Bible is the book that addresses these questions head on, directly, and with sustaining relevance.

A story

Jill frankly could not see much point in the Bible. It seemed an inglorious waste of time. She had children, she had bills to pay, she had dishes to clean, places to be—there were not enough hours in the day to do what she needed to accomplish. Studying the Bible was fine when she was a student, but now that she had grown up a little and had the busy demands of home life thrust upon her, she found she had no space or time to read the Bible. She didn't miss it. She thought she had what she needed to do what she needed to do, and she had no more time to read theoretical statements about how to be more holy. Phew, time to do more cleaning.

But then one day a friend suggested that she simply read a proverb first thing in the morning. Before long she found that she was learning—and not simply learning, She was, well, being 'fed'. The way she looked at things, the way she did things, her mood and patience with her family and friends, all that began to be changed. Strangely, though she had added one more thing to her schedule, she now felt less busy, not more busy. Things were being put in perspective, and she was focusing on what mattered most of all, God.

Questions for discussion

1. What sort of problems are you facing at the moment?

2. Do you think the Bible has anything to say about those problems?

3. Where do you think the Bible addresses those issues?

4. What could you do to read what the Bible has to say about the issues you are facing?

5. What do you think the Bible is primarily concerned about?

Is the Bible Interesting?

Now there's a question! You would think that the answer that most Christians would give would be a definitive 'yes', but as I observe patterns of behavior, I do wonder. How much time do we spend reading the Bible, watching TV, studying the Bible, studying our smart phones? The comparisons suggest more than merely which of these two kinds of behavior we actually find more interesting. Just because I spend more time at work than I do studying the Bible (or going to the movies) does not necessarily mean that I find work more interesting than the Bible (or than going to the movies). Nonetheless, it is suggestive, as is the tendency for us to look for a church or preacher who can – oh, so difficult a task! – bring the Bible to 'life'. As if without the skilled incantations of a magician, the thing is a lifeless husk of interest only to specialists, like a Shakespearian sonnet (with apologies to lovers of The Bard everywhere!).

The Bible is interesting because God is interesting

If we approach the Bible as merely a book (a book that we read as any other book), or more accurately a collection of books, then, if we like books, stories, poetry, history, we are likely to find the Bible interesting. But if we do not like them, we are unlikely to find it interesting. Suppose you discover in your basement an old letter. Say it is from someone you have never heard of who left it there by mistake, perhaps being the property of a previous owner of the house. You might wonder for a moment whether you should read the letter, given it was not addressed to you, but you are not likely to want to spend the rest of your life reading it. But suppose, instead, you discover in a corner of your house a letter written by your wife, now deceased, or a letter from a girlfriend or boyfriend that had somehow been misplaced. Whether or not the letter is well written, whether or not it has literary or historical merits, you are now interested. Why? Because the person who wrote it interests you. Foundationally, the Bible is interesting because God is interesting.

Certainly, the human authors of the book have interest as well. Who could be more fascinating than, say, David? David was at the same time the greatest general and the greatest musician, as well as being the greatest political leader of his age. This is quite a beguiling combination! Who else in history has been able to lead like Winston Churchill, sing like Paul McCartney, and fight like the Duke of Wellington? So to read poems and speeches by David, and to read about David is itself intrinsically interesting. But it is only interesting if you are interested in politics, music, and warfare—and in particular if you are interested in the history of those things. There is definitely a market for that; think of all the biographies of the great American presidents and the founding fathers. But the Bible is far more than a record of great people doing great deeds in the distant past. The Bible is interesting, not just because its human authors are interesting, but because its divine author is interesting. What could be more fascinating than the creator of the whole universe? Everything good, beautiful, exciting, fulfilling, joyful, beneficial, and dangerous (yes, that too) is summed up, and infinitely surpassed, in this person that the Bible is about: God.

The Bible is interesting because God is interested in you

Think of the Bible as a love letter from your Lover, a fatherly letter from your Father, a friend's letter from your Friend, a personal summons to a small intimate dinner party at Buckingham Palace from your Queen. It is written to *you*. Now, there are various interpretative guidelines we need to have in mind when we read the Bible – the Bible is not *about* you, even if it is *to* you – and we will address those guidelines in chapter 5, 'How Do You Read the Bible?' But do not mistake the fact that the Bible is 'living and active' and from God to you. The Bible is interesting not only because God is interesting, but also because this God is interested in you. Being 'God-centered' in our approach to the Bible and life means being centered on the God who is— and part of the reality of God is that He loves His people. Ask yourself this: Why else would God have caused the Bible to be written if it was not for the fact that He loves the people to whom it was written? Do you think God needed to write the Bible to communicate to Himself? The Bible is *about* God, but it is not *to* God. It is written to you. When you pick up the Bible to read it, then, if you do so with an open heart and mind, trustingly, with a desire to hear and obey, then you will have the amazing experience that Samuel had: Speak, Lord, for your servant hears (1 Sam. 3:9). Say that truly, and you will find that He speaks in the Bible *to* you.

There are, again, various tools and techniques that can help in interpreting the Bible rightly (and prevent you from interpreting the Bible wrongly), but there is a danger here. Sometimes these tools can be employed in such a way that we almost take the Bible out of people's hands and put it back in the hands of the experts. God is a speaking God, and by His Spirit He breathed out the Bible, and by His Spirit He illumines the hearts and minds of those who faithfully read the Bible. Many times I have found that the most insightful interpretations of the Bible have come from the simple reader of the Bible, often without advanced degrees in biblical interpretation, but with an honest and humble desire to hear from God. Why? God is interested in us. And so the Bible is interesting because God is interesting and because God is interested in you.

The Bible is interesting because God has designed the Bible to be your food

'Man shall not live by bread alone, but by every word that comes from the mouth of God,' Jesus quoted to answer the devil's temptations at the start of Jesus' ministry (Matt. 4:4; cf. Deut. 8:3). These words are your life, peace and health (Prov. 4:22). They are eternal life. 'You have the words of eternal life,' as Jesus' disciple Peter said of Jesus (John 6:68). Meditate on them day and night; then you will be prosperous and successful, as God told Joshua at the start of his leadership (Josh. 1:8).

People think of the Bible far too much as a repository of information (spiritual/religious). If that were the case, then the great question to ask of the Bible would be the educational question. How much of it do we remember after we have finished reading it? How much of it have we managed to put into practice in our lives a certain amount of time after having read the Bible? The answer to those questions can be encouraging for those who believe in the importance of the Bible, and can also be discouraging. We have brought in various studies and ideas about how people learn, whether people are visual or auditory learners, and whether certain people learn from books or learn by experience. But all this is quite wrong-headed. The Bible is not a repository of spiritual/religious information.

The Bible is *food*. Spiritual food, to be sure. No one is meant physically to eat the Bible! But it is food, nonetheless. The great question to ask about food is not, 'What do you remember about what you ate yesterday?' Sometimes you can remember what you ate; sometimes you cannot. The great thing is to eat it. You will notice that if you do not eat it, you will grow gradually weaker— physically weaker if we are talking about physical food, spiritually weaker if we are talking about the Bible. As a person grows into being an adult, they need more food to nourish their growth spurt. Without appropriate nutrients, they stultify and do not reach their full potential.

The great reason why the Western church does not see the kind of impact, maturity, and growth in every season that it longs for, is because it has lost this notion of the Bible as spiritual nourishment. It views the Bible as an information source, not a nourishing source. It views it as a lecture, not as a meal. It views it as a technique, not a power to make a change in someone's life.

But the Bible is food or, to switch metaphor, it is a seed. A seed, when planted in good soil (receptive, faithful, human hearts), will gradually grow more and more to become a strong tree—as long as it is not strangled by the thorns of worldly cares. Whether the farmer sleeps or is awake, the seed grows (Mark 4:27). There is an intrinsic power in this Bible, a power that is not present in a lesson about mathematics or literature or history. The Bible is interesting because God has designed the Bible to be your food.

These three principles – the Bible is interesting because God is interesting, because God is interested in you, and because God has designed the Bible to be your food – should prevent you from ever finding the Bible anything other than extraordinarily (supernaturally) fascinating.

A story

Jerry did not dare admit it to his Christians friends, but he found the Bible dull. Boring, even. It was hard for him to stay awake during sermons, and he only ever perked up during an illustration or amusing anecdote. He liked the music, and he quite enjoyed the architecture. But whenever the Bible was opened it was all he could do to stifle a yawn. It was the same at home: his Bible was covered in dust. All along throughout his life he had found book learning difficult. He had been the sort of person who had wanted to learn by doing, not by sitting in a library. He was brilliant with multimedia, and video. But books left him cold.

One day he dared to mention this problem to his pastor. The pastor thought for a moment and said, 'You know what your problem is?' Jerry looked warily at the pastor expecting some sort of stern rebuke. 'Your problem is that you don't know what the Bible is.' Jerry was confused. 'Of course, I know what the Bible is. It's a book.' 'No,' said his pastor, 'It's not. It's food.' Jerry wasn't sure that this different way of looking at the Bible would make a whole lot of difference.

But the next time he came to read the Bible, he decided that instead of asking God that he would learn something new, he would ask God to feed his soul. Strangely enough, that morning he didn't learn anything new. But he did have a new meeting with a Person. And bit by bit Jerry started to become new himself.

Questions for discussion

1. Do you find the Bible interesting?

2. Do you find God interesting?

3. Would you be interested in reading what God is saying to you now?

4. Would you be interested in receiving a spiritual nourishment that would feed your very soul?

5. What could you do to read the Bible as food for your life?

Is the Bible Authoritative?

Of course, Christians want to immediately answer that question with a resounding yes! If Christians are anything, they are people who believe that the Bible is an important book. While the term 'authoritative' might not be exactly the sort of way of phrasing it that some would like – it sounds a little too close to 'authoritarian', which of course carries negative connotations – it captures the essence of the commonly-held view. The Bible is The Book par excellence—the word 'Bible' means 'Book', as in the only Book that really counts!

But scratch a little beneath the surface and the question becomes more tricky. In what sense is it authoritative? Is it always authoritative in every situation? And if so, what sanctioned interpretation of it should we take to be authoritative—and what authoritatively-sanctioned interpretations of the interpretation? Quite quickly it becomes difficult to know exactly what it is that we are talking about when we talk about the 'authority' of the Bible.

How are we to interpret the narrative portions of the Bible? For instance, are we meant to take the Israelite conquest as a model for contemporary military action? And if the answer to that is no, then why not? And are we merely spiritualizing the conquest when we interpret it in terms of spiritual or moral warfare? If we are to take the instructional parts of the Bible more literally (that word 'literal' is one that needs to be defined carefully too, by the way), then is that true of all of them? For instance, are we meant to celebrate the Sabbath in the way that they did in the Old Testament—and if not, why not? And why that apparent 'exception' when others (such as adultery) are not viewed in the same exceptional terms? It is not surprising that after a while some people today just throw up their hands and treat the Bible as a sort of collection of Instagram fortune cookies, best thoughts for the day, or else avoid reading it altogether.

In chapter 1, I have already looked at the truthfulness of Scripture, which, of course, overlaps with (though is distinct from) a claim to its authority. In that chapter, I briefly outlined what I call the Jesus defence of the truthfulness of Scripture. The same approach works for its authority—but there is more to be said, too.

Focus on the Author (and not just the authors)

Indubitably, the Bible is a book that is authored by humans. This is what makes it so different from, say, the Koran. While the Koran claims to have landed in Mohammed's lap like a slab of spiritual dynamite from heaven, the Bible does not make any such claim to its inspiration. Men spoke from God as they were inspired by the Holy Spirit (2 Pet. 1:21). All Scripture is inspired by God or God-breathed (2 Tim. 3:16). There are, then, human personalities.

There are different 'genres' (or kinds of writing, like poetry, history, or law). There is a wide historical range of writings, from which different backgrounds influence the genre and the human personalities that are writing the words that you read. The rediscovery or, really, re-emphasis of this human side of the Bible is no bad thing. If we think the Bible is like the Koran, we will misunderstand the Bible in all sorts of important ways.

The Bible is *designed* to be (if you like) *incarnate*. It is both fully human *and also* fully divine. This means that it can be assessed, studied, interpreted, and is more accessible and real than a wooden, one-toned book. You must bring your human sensibilities to the Bible as you read it, focusing on the human authors.

But if you *only* read it that way, you will miss its larger claim. The Bible does claim that it is God-inspired. Apart from the well-known quotation of 2 Timothy 3:16, we could also point out the way Jesus treats Scripture. He does not only treat the Old Testament where God is 'quoted' as being something that God says, but the whole thing – even the editorial comments of the Old Testament – are equally inspired. Note the reasoning of Matthew 19:4-5. Jesus quotes the (human) authorial comment of Genesis 2:24 as something that the Creator said. He also promises that His appointed apostles will have the capacity by the Spirit to remember and recall the truth of Jesus, and so write the New Testament (John 14:26).

Having identified that larger claim, and having put your trust in Jesus, who, as your Lord makes that claim, now think: what does that mean about this book that I read? If my Lord treated it as authoritative, then should I not also?

Taste and see

There is plentiful warning in the Bible against putting God to the test. But there is also plentiful encouragement to have what the Puritans called 'experimental religion'. That is not to 'experiment' with God, but to experience God. In the end, we can put together many different intellectual arguments for the experience of the Bible speaking to us—and such intellectual arguments are important lest we fall into the trap of merely believing in the Bible for subjective or emotional causes.

But the experience of the Bible speaking to us is far more than merely an intellectual conclusion. And having the Author address us through His Word is not just a response to a lengthy treatise about authority. I in no way wish to encourage you to 'check your brain at the door' when you read the Bible. Certainly, ask questions. Certainly, engage your brain. But, first of all, try the Bible on for size. Come to it in a spirit of humility, willing and open to have the Author authoritatively address you directly through His Word. As Jesus put it, 'My sheep hear my voice, and I know them, and they follow me' (John 10:27). That is not counter-rational, but it is not merely rational either.

Remember the character of the Author

When we think of *authority*, we tend to think of someone who is telling us what to do in a slightly high-handed and insensitive way. But remember the character of the Author. This is your Creator who knows you better than you know yourself, who has dreams for you, who has known you since before the creation of the world (Eph. 1:4): the one whose purpose for you is glory and pleasures forevermore at His right hand (Ps. 16:11); who delights over you and sings over you (Zeph. 3:17); who loves you with an everlasting love (Jer. 31:3); who gave His Son for you (John 3:16); whose plan for you is peace and good, and everything working together, albeit sometimes mysteriously, for that good (Rom. 8:28). If you ever doubt His love, look at the cross. 'God demonstrates his own love for us in this: while we were still sinners, Christ died for us' (Rom. 5:8 NIV).

Recognize the role of the church, but don't overplay that role

God has given teachers to the church, both present and in the past, and it makes sense to listen carefully to their interpretations of the Bible. The Bible is not always a simple book. Why should we assume that it would be? If nuclear physics is a difficult subject to grasp, are we surprised if the Creator of the universe is beyond the grasp of simplistic expressions? Some parts of the Bible are relatively straightforward. Others are more difficult. But either way it makes sense to listen carefully to God-appointed, holy, and humble preachers and teachers who can help us make sense of the Bible and how it applies to our own lives.

While we are to recognize the role of the church, however, we are not to overplay it. Some Christians have thought that the best way to safeguard the authority of the Bible, and protect us against false interpretations, is to cede their interpretative abilities entirely to the church. But, of course, this just moves the problem one stage back. Who is to interpret the church's interpreters? Keep the authority invested in the authority of the Bible itself. While the church played, and still plays, a role in recognizing the

Bible's canonical authority, it is not the Author Himself. Think of it the way that an expert recognizes a work of art, say a Van Gogh. An art expert can discern whether a particular painting is by Van Gogh or is a fake. Similarly, the church has had a role to play in discerning what are the right books to include in the Bible, writing as the human authors of the Bible, and teaching the Bible to subsequent generations. But no one confuses an art expert who recognizes a Van Gogh with Van Gogh.

Use your reason, but don't worship your mind

Your mind is important in reading the Bible. It might be thought that to accept the authority of the Bible means throwing your brain away and accepting everything it says brainlessly. Nothing could be further from the truth. Christianity has always been a religion of *light*, and where it has flourished, people have *thought*, developed *thinking*, founded universities and hospitals, and the like. In fact, unless you are willing to ask some hard questions, you probably won't be able to accept the authority of the Bible.

To listen to, receive, and begin to understand what the Author says will require every brain cell you have and then some more. You must use your mind; you must ask questions; you must enquire, read, think, and read some more. But that is different from worshipping your mind. An atheist, it has been said, is a person who thinks that God can be contained within the confines of his own mind. Instead, you must be in a position where you are ready for your mind to be expanded, grown, and developed as you start to use it more and more to get to grips with what the Author is saying to you.

Pray for illumination

When we read the Bible, we are reading it, if doing so faithfully, in a way that is in conscious dependence upon God to illumine His Word. Paul indicates as much to Timothy when he says that Timothy is to 'think over' what Paul says, 'for the Lord will give you understanding in everything' (2 Tim. 2:7). John assumes the same work of the Holy Spirit in granting the Christian understanding and insight when he says that disciples have an 'anointing' that 'teaches you about everything' (1 John 2:27). This is in fulfillment of Jesus' promise that His disciples would receive the Holy Spirit and the Holy Spirit will 'teach you all things' (John 14:26)—a promise fulfilled primarily in the divine inspiration given to the apostles to be authors and guarantors of the New Testament, but secondarily fulfilled in the work of the Holy Spirit in illumining the reading of the Bible.

Because God has designed His Word so that it is inspired by God, as well as authored by humans – it is authored by God completely and fully too – this means that to understand it, we need the work of God Himself. We are therefore to pray for the illumination of God; He is the Author, and if we are to hear from Him, then He must speak. 'Speak, Lord, for your servant hears' is not only to be the prayer of a youthful Samuel (1 Sam. 3:9-10), but also of every faithful disciple. As the psalmist famously prays: 'Open my eyes, that I may behold wondrous things out of your law' (Ps. 119:18).

A story

John was truly interested in the Bible, read the Bible, and wanted to center his life upon what it said. But then something awkward happened. He was in a relationship with a person that became intimate—in ways that the Bible clearly spoke of as sinful. What was he to do? To be honest, his actions did not feel sinful at all. Quite the contrary; they felt good. But because John knew the Bible pretty well, he knew what it had to say about what he was doing. Was John going to submit to the authority of the Bible, or was he going to submit the Bible to the authority of his own personal experience?

He read around on the Internet about what other Christians had done with the same feelings. To his surprise he found quite a lot had developed sophisticated-sounding 'theologies' which were attempting to claim biblical warrant for what they were doing; John knew all that was bogus. If they hadn't felt what they had felt, they wouldn't have developed their 'theologies'! It was quite clear that it was their experience that was in the driver's seat, not the Bible.

John decided he was going to be honest. Either keep doing what he was doing and reject the Bible, or stop doing what he was doing. He remembered what Peter had said about Jesus: 'You have the words of eternal life.' John realized that something more important was at stake than merely his own experience. It was his life, now and forever. Hesitantly at first, and imperfectly, John submitted to the Bible's authority in every area of his life once again. Surprisingly, he discovered that bit by bit he was now actually experiencing fullness of life. The Author of the Bible was the greatest experience ever – and was experienced as John accepted the Author's authority.

Questions for discussion

1. Have you ever had something happen that made you question the authority of the Bible?

2. What parts of the Bible do you find difficult to submit to?

3. Do you think God's authority is a good authority?

4. Are there things in your past which when you look back you find that God was right, even if at the time you found it hard to believe that He knew what He was doing?

5. Is there freedom in submitting to the one who wants to set you free?

QUESTION 5

How Do You Read the Bible?

The interpretation of the Bible is a matter not only fraught with difficulties in theory, but one whose right practice depends upon your foundational understanding of what the Bible *is*. In some ways, if our understanding of the Bible's authority (see chapter 4) is anything less than accurate, it will almost inevitably mean that our interpretation of the Bible is likely to be similarly inaccurate. We read a poem written by an unknown author in a different way than one written by our lover, and we read a sentence to incarceration recorded in a court of law in a different way than hearing that sentence directly delivered to us by a judge. What is more, *reading* the Bible is more than simply knowing how to interpret it accurately. It includes practical methods, some of which are helpful for most people in most places, and others which might be particular to an individual's own pattern of life. We all need to eat food, and there certainly is a wrong way to eat food, but being too prescriptive about the time at which one should eat breakfast is likely to come across as being dictatorial, petty, and the sort of advice more honoured in the breach than in the observance.

The following are by no means exhaustive how-to approaches to reading the Bible, but at the same time, if they are followed, they will keep you from the more egregious errors and will also tend towards inculcating a life-long habit of Bible reading that will nourish your soul and honor God.

Remember the Bible is not primarily about you

That the Bible is not primarily about you is different from saying that the Bible is not relevant to you, or not spoken to you. If the Bible is God speaking, then it would be pointless to have such communication if there were not intended hearers at the other end of such communication. The Bible is *to* you, but it is still not *about* you. In other words, you are not the hero of the story. This comes as quite a shock at first, and remains a fairly sizeable pill to swallow for some of us all of our lives, but it is absolutely essential for us to realize this if we are to get anywhere at all. This is the root cause of many of the worst interpretative blunders that are commonly made, as well as some of the subtler ones.

At the extreme end, every time you see a Bible verse ripped dramatically out of context and stuck on a poster and then affixed to a wall, you can be fairly sure that the mind, thinking or worldview behind it has not stopped to consider the Bible as not being primarily *about* us. For instance, 'I can do all things through Christ who strengthens me' (Phil. 4:13) stuck to the wall of a workout gym is not by itself an evil thing to do. But it is so badly misrepresenting the meaning of that text that it becomes silly, therefore undermining the important message that that text does carry. But then at the other more subtle end of interpretative blunders, the perennial attempt by academics to develop a 'theology' of this or that, in order to answer the questions of our day, can fall into a similar, if more sophisticated, trap. Why should we let the Bible's message be dictated by developing a 'theology' of (for instance) environmentalism. To be sure, the Bible does have things to say about the environment (or, better to say, 'creation'), but the way the question is asked, and the way the answer is formed, suggests that the dominating character in the story is always our own concern, our agenda, our framework—into which we are trying to find a clever way to fit the Bible. In fact, on occasion I wonder whether some 'theologies' (don't you love the plural form?) are really little more than 'human-ologies', dictated by the concerns and desires of one particular group of humans at one particular time.

The Bible is primarily a rescue message

We are taking the bird's-eye, big-picture view here: if you look down at the Great Wall of China from high up (apparently it is one of the few, if not only, human-made structures you can see from outer space), the most important thing to notice about it is that it is a wall. And a wall is designed either to keep people (or animals) out, or to keep people (or animals) in, or both. In other words, at its most basic, the Great Wall of China is a wall that is a barrier designed to separate one group of people from another group of people. Of course, the Great Wall of China is many other things too. It is a cultural statement of extraordinary power; a massively brilliant work of human engineering; and a relatively ineffective defensive fortress. It is made of a zillion (or thereabouts) stones, etc. etc. But the first thing to get straight in your mind is that the Great Wall of China is a *wall*.

Similarly, the first thing for us to get straight, or keep straight, in our mind about the Bible when we come to read it is that it is a *rescue* message. It tells a story (though the Bible is not always narrative, so it is better to say it sends a message) of how God intends to rescue His creation. That is its controlling message throughout, all the way through, from beginning to end. The Bible starts in paradise (Eden), descends into rebellion (the fall of Adam and Eve), culminates in the cross (God's rescue mission), and is completed in the New Heaven and the New Earth (return to paradise). For sure, there is a lot more to say about the Bible than just that, but it is important we keep that basic infrastructure and framework very clear in our minds as we read it.

The Bible is written in many different styles

Genre is the kind of writing in which the book we are reading is written—'genre' comes from the Latin 'genus' meaning the style or type or kind of a thing. Sensitivity to 'genre' impacts how we are to read the book. This seems so obvious that one is almost embarrassed to labor the point, but ignorance of it, wilful or inadvertent, has led to such serious errors that apparently it does have to be underlined. When the Bible says in a psalm that the sun 'rises' and 'sets', it is not making a claim for the geocentric nature of the universe. That would be like interpreting William Wordsworth's famous line 'I wandered lonely as a cloud' to mean that he thought that human beings were made of the same material as a cloud. Poetry must be interpreted by the rules of poetry. This brings up the whole, much-vexed notion of whether the Bible is to be taken *literally*. The trouble with this question is that it begs another: what does it mean to take anything literally? Of course, as soon as you ask that, it is not too long before you are tarred and feathered as being a radical and subjectivist. But sensitivity to the style, tone, and type of communication is absolutely basic to all communications. One wonders whether people who hate the idea of even asking what it means to take something literally have any sense of humor at all. All too often you find that they do not have much of one. That is, they treat all communication as the kind of communication of which they are most familiar and like the best. A form of legal instructions, most likely. You also wonder what sort of poetry – or history, or novels, or songs – these people write. 'Literal' in this conversation seems to mean: should you interpret the Bible as if every part of it were a legal or scientific instruction? The answer to that of course is no! For ironically enough, if you did interpret every part of the Bible as a legal instruction, you would not be interpreting it literally—for it literally is not intended all to be taken literally. It is better to think of the Bible as a collection of books, with different styles, and therefore the reader's job is to interpret it as the author (and Author) intends.

Avoid the application fallacy

Every Bible study group I have been a part of, observed, heard of, or overseen, has had a tendency to make one of two mistakes with regard to application, and each are born of what I call the 'application fallacy'.

Some people when they read the Bible make almost no effort whatsoever to consider whether the Bible passage they are reading might mean anything to them individually. Such people are rare these days for we tend to be so 'me-centered' – see the principle above about the Bible not being about us – that we have a leaning towards assuming that anything we read has something to do with us. (This, of course, is why we are so sensitive towards any, even unintentional, slight. As the quip goes, 'When I was young, I thought everyone was thinking about me; when I was older, I realized they weren't thinking about me as much as I had assumed; when I was older still, I realized that they hadn't even been thinking about me at all'!) It is possible, certainly in university settings, to read the Bible as if it were a mere work of history or a literary artefact.

On the other hand, more commonly, there are people who read the Bible and very quickly, if not immediately, make a jump to assuming that what the Bible is saying there has direct application to them today.

In either case, there is at play the 'application fallacy'. This fallacy is the thought that *we* must do the application if it is to happen at all. The thinking goes like this. Here is a Bible verse on love. Well, that is all very well, how interesting. And there the thinking stops if there is no attempt at application at all. But if there is an attempt at application, the leap comes into play. Well, that is about love, but what on earth is the application? We must apply this text! For some reason or other the idea that a Bible text about how we are to love each other might be best applied by us loving each other does not enter into the heads of many people. I put it like this: if we take the time to listen carefully to what the Bible *was* saying in its original context and to its original audience, nine times out of ten, the meaning and application of the Bible passage for us today will become embarrassingly, plainly obvious.

First, we need to understand what the Bible said then.[1] After that we need to understand what that passage means. Once we have done that, we will find that the application, what it means to us, will be fairly obvious most of the time. 'What does it say?' is the first question. Then, 'what does it mean?' After that should come, 'what does it mean to me?' Too often people jump over the first two steps ('what does it say?' and 'what does it mean?') in a commendable attempt to get practical or make this thing applicable, and by doing so actually miss the obvious application of the passage! Why? Because they haven't understood in the first place what the passage is saying and what it means. Once we do that, we will be able to apply it, usually, quite straightforwardly.

A story

Bridget had found reading the Bible a tricky habit to keep. She knew that she was meant to read it, but too often she found the time slipping away before she got around to actually sitting down with her Bible open and reading it. When you asked her why, it was not a matter of business or scheduling. For her it seemed as if reading the Bible was reading a work of literature or history— fascinating to be sure, if you liked that kind of thing. Plus, she felt sure that it would just be telling her what to do and what not to do. And she found it hard enough to keep up with the things she already knew she was meant to be doing without adding anything else to the list—especially not every single day!

---

1   These questions are further explained in the next chapter.

But then, when she was talking about this with a friend, she realized that reading the Bible was reading a message from God to her. That made her approach it with a quite different attitude. Now she wanted to find out what God was saying to her each morning. She also began to realize, as she read it more and more, that it was not just a list of do's and don'ts. 'Grace' was the word that came to her mind when she now thought about the Bible.

Questions for discussion

1. What difference does it make to your approach to reading the Bible to realize that the Bible is not primarily *about* you?

2. How would you read the Bible differently if you read it as a message from God *to* you'?

3. Do you tend to apply the Bible to your life too quickly or not to apply it at all?

4. When you think of the Bible, do you think of something that weighs you down or something that lifts you up?

5. How could you become more effective at reading the Bible with a sensitivity to genre or its style of writing?

When Do You Read the Bible?

This question is often born more of frustration than anything else. When on earth can I find the time to read the Bible? There is so much going on; I have so many responsibilities; I am inculcated with endless distractions from people demanding one thing or another from me. When, in the name of all that is holy, can I find the time and space to sit down and have a so-called 'quiet time'?

It is certainly a fair question. One anecdote from the life of the Welsh preacher Martyn Lloyd-Jones helps illuminate the challenges on the other side of the way the question has been posed. Giving a talk to a group of medical students, Lloyd-Jones was asked how it was possible for a medical student to find the time to have a daily space to read the Bible. Waxing lyrical for a while, and driving home the necessity of daily Bible reading, Lloyd-Jones said that he only made one exception to this rule: the mothers of nursing children. For all others, in all other situations, there should be a way to find time to read the Bible.

That has certainly been my experience. If I can find time to eat, I can find time to read the Bible. If I can find time to go to the bathroom, I can find time to read the Bible (and also thereby a quiet space to read the Bible too). There are, if we are honest with ourselves, far too many excuses made for not reading the Bible which, when examined under the cold, clear light of day, do not stand up as being valid. Busy? Are you too busy to have a shower, too busy to eat a slice of bread? But if the Bible is your life and man does not live by bread alone, surely you have time to read the Bible if you have time to wash and eat. And, again, if we are being frank, many of us spend hours a day whittling away our time in entertainment and screen time, television, Internet surfing, social media, and the rest.

To simply come back, however, and say the problem is not time, but how we use our time, is not particularly helpful. Presumably, the person asking this question needs help with knowing when to read the Bible, and how to carve out the space to read it each day. The following, then, are key principles and practices that over and over again I have found have been helpful to people to answer this question.

Start small

So many times people think that if they are going to commit to reading the Bible each day, they need to carve out at least an hour and study the Bible with all sorts of commentaries and special extra help. But I say: start small. Five minutes is better, far better, than nothing. Don't read what I'm writing here and say, 'Well, okay, now I'm going to read the Bible,' and begin by carving out three hours, having a mammoth Bible reading marathon, and then finding the next day you cannot be bothered anymore. Start small.

Commit to read the Bible five minutes each day. Better little and often than eating a spiritual meal only once a week.

Start early

I fully understand that some people find it easy to get up early and other people do not, that some people are morning people and some are not. It is also true that there are many people I know who have made a successful habit of reading the Bible last thing at night. But, my guess is, if you are asking this question, then you have not made a successful habit of reading the Bible last thing at night. To do so requires an inbuilt pattern generated over years. It is easier to just go to sleep; plus, you are tired; plus, you have had a long day. You get the idea. The advantage of reading the Bible first thing in the morning is that you cannot forget to do it; cannot put it off and cannot delay it; you cannot get distracted. Place the Bible on the nightstand next to your bed, or on the floor next to your camp bed; when you wake up, turn on the light, reach for the Bible, and before your feet hit the floor start to read the thing. Start early.

Pray first

Reading the Bible is a spiritual exercise. We need to ask God to illumine His Word so that we can hear what He is saying to us. Reading the Bible is not simply an exercise in learning more about God. It is meant to be a time when we can actually hear from God ourselves. Therefore, ask God to speak to you: Open my eyes, that I may behold wondrous things out of your law (Ps. 119:18); speak, Lord, for your servant hears (1 Sam. 3:9); Lord, your sheep hear your voice and they follow you (John 10:27); help me to hear your voice and follow what it is that you say to me.

The single most important transformative habit that you can introduce, if you have not already, is to pray before you read the Bible. Remember, God speaks through His Word. You are wanting to hear from God. Therefore, ask God to speak to you that morning as you read.

Use a tool to help keep you on track

There are so many of these tools nowadays that we are really spoiled for choice. One of the oldest and best is Robert Murray M'Cheyne's Bible-in-a-year reading plan. But if you use this excellent tool you will not be reading only a small part of the Bible. Because M'Cheyne takes you through the Bible in one year, it necessitates reading large chunks of the Bible each day. You may be able to handle that, or you may not. If not, don't use M'Cheyne, use one of today's excellent Bible guides. I write a daily guide along these lines called 'God Centered Bible' which is available at *Godcenteredlife.org* and can appear automatically each morning in your email inbox.

The point is that you don't want to rely on your own native initiative to decide all the time which part of the Bible to read next. If you do that, you may end up only reading the parts that you already like or, alternatively, only reading the parts that you find confusing and want to understand. But whether you are reading Philippians over and over again, or similarly the book of Revelation, it is important instead to, as much as possible, eat a balanced diet, spiritually as much as physically. A Bible guide as a tool can help you do this.

Actually read the Bible

This seems a strange thing to emphasize, but I have found it to be true with people I talk to. Having a 'devotional' is not the same if you only read what someone else says about the Bible, rather than the Bible itself. The point of a quiet time or 'devotional' is to spend time reading the Bible yourself. Certainly, someone else's thoughts or comments can help. But this is not meant to be like listening to another sermon. You will not grow to maturity yourself unless you learn to hear from God yourself, and that means actually reading the Bible yourself. Read it. Think about it. Ask questions about it. Take the joyful risk of plunging into the water yourself, and not just reading about how someone else has taken the plunge. Don't just read a travel guide to that exciting part of the world you've always wanted to visit; actually also go there for yourself and explore for yourself. Don't just read about the Bible; actually read the Bible too. It's far more exciting than secondhand comments on the Bible.

Ask three crucial questions, and ask them in the order 1-2-3

First of all, ask, 'What does it say?' That is, you need to read the Bible passage, probably read it again, and ask and answer the question as to what this passage is actually saying. How would you summarize it in a sentence? Then ask the next question, which is, 'What does it mean?' This is different from the question about what it says because now you are seeking to discern the intention of the passage in front of you. For instance, you may be reading about how Paul went to Corinth, preached there, was brought in front of the Roman tribunal, but the case was dismissed by Gallio (Acts 18). That is what the passage *says*. But what does it *mean*? Why did Luke include this part of the story? There are lots of other details in Paul's life he could have included; why this part?

It is important to ask this question because it prevents us from making what otherwise would be gross errors. For instance, the passage to which we have just referred, where Paul was dragged before a Roman tribunal, presumably does not mean that all preachers will at some point be dragged before a court. But unless you ask the question, 'What does it mean?' you can jump from description ('What does it say?') to application ('What does it mean to me?') bypassing intention ('What does it mean?') and so end up with some unhappy and unfortunate application takeaways. By the way, the passage probably means something along the lines that Luke is showing how the Christian faith was accepted as legal by the Roman authorities at the time.

We have one other final question to ask, however. That is, 'What does it mean to me?' This is the much-vexed 'application' question. It must be asked *last*. You cannot ask the application question until you have asked both the description question and then the intention question. If you attempt to find an application before you have asked those other two questions, you will misapply the text.

For instance, the passage we mentioned above (Acts 18) describes how Paul in this instance said nothing because Gallio intervened to protect him. Given that, unless you ask the description and intention questions first, you could jump to the conclusion that the application is to stay quiet when someone accuses you. Does not Jesus say to turn the other cheek

(Matt. 5:39)? Was He not Himself silent before His trial (Luke 23:9)? I can feel a pretty good sermon brewing! But, no, the application, if taken after asking, 'What does it say?' and then, 'What does it mean?' will in most instances fairly naturally emerge. In this case the application might be something along the lines that even in a pagan society, the gospel of Jesus Christ is powerful and effective; therefore, keep on speaking and teaching about Jesus—which is actually what Jesus had specifically told Paul beforehand (Acts 18:9-10). Then to apply that to your situation might mean something like, 'I need to take fresh courage to share my faith today.' Asking these three questions, and in order, might initially seem cumbersome, but in time to come will flow naturally—just make sure you don't become lazy and jump straight to number three!

Pray last

Having read the Bible and discerned what God is saying to you today, you then want to make a commitment to follow through and do what He is saying. Is there a command to obey? A promise to trust? A truth to believe? A hope to hold onto? An assurance to enjoy? A peace to receive? But before you put these wondrous truths into practice, you need to ask for God's help. Spiritual change is possible, but it requires spiritual power. So then having asked God to speak to you, having discerned what He is saying, you now need to ask God for the help to do what He is saying.

A story

Emma knew that she should read the Bible, but somehow or other she never found the time to do so. One day her small group leader pointed out to her that she seemed to find the time for a lot of other things: friends, family, food, even TV. What about God? Emma was a little taken aback by the directness of the question. But when she went home and thought about it she realized that her group leader was making a valid point. If she really was claiming that the reason why she was not reading the Bible was because she was busy, then how was it that she was not too busy to spend an hour a day watching TV? Convicted by the realization that her reason was really an excuse, Emma asked her Bible study leader for advice on reading the Bible and when to do so. The answer surprised Emma. She had expected to be loaded down with a very demanding schedule and all sorts of lengthy theoretical techniques. But instead, the group leader simply told Emma to start small. Five minutes a day should do it to begin with, she advised. Start early, first thing in the morning. And don't forget to ask God to speak to you and ask Him for His help to put into practice what He said.

Questions for discussion

1. Have you ever found it hard to keep up a regular pattern of daily Bible reading?

2. What time of day do you find it most helpful to read the Bible?

3. What did God say to you most recently when you read the Bible?

4. What tools have you found helpful in your Bible reading?

5. Do you think you are too busy to read the Bible?

Does it Matter if We Use the Bible in Church?

It is not that uncommon today to go to church and hear very little about the Bible during the actual worship services. The reason for this is because some Christian leaders are of the opinion that the Bible – as it stands, and written in the way and in the order in which it was written – is off-putting to those who are unfamiliar with church today. We are, it is often said, in a post-literate culture. We live today primarily in a 'visual' culture, and the Bible is, of course, primarily a 'verbal' piece of communication. People, it is said, do not read as much as they used to, and so to have a book (albeit, Christians would say, 'The Book') playing a prominent role in church worship services is an unnecessary and immediate turnoff.

Therefore, while most, if not all, Christians recognize the authority of the Scriptures in some sense or other, there are many Christian leaders who are aiming to fashion their church services with the Bible somewhat marginalized. If the Bible is quoted, the quotations will appear in brief soundbite form, perhaps depicted on a video screen. Rarely will a particular part of the Bible be studied in context—the very word 'studied' also seems to such folk to be an unnecessary and immediate turnoff today. But if it is used at all, the Bible verses will be removed from their original context and presented as a string of examples, or proofs, to make a more accessible, practical, and relevant point as part of the overall communication.

I want to argue that all that is seriously mistaken, but as I do so, I realize that I am swimming upstream. So before I merrily plunge in and start thrashing about trying to make headway against the current, pushing in the other direction, I think it prudent to see if I can make a few preliminary points that will, if not jet propel the conversation forward, at least provide some extra initial momentum.

The first point would be that it is fallacious to argue that we are living in a non-literate society when compared to the society in which the Bible was originally written. Of course, the Bible was written over a long period of time, but all historians would agree that for most of those years in which it was written, the majority of people could not read. Yes, you heard that correctly: the Bible was itself written in a primarily non-literate society. When today we say 'post-literate,' we do not mean that most people today literally cannot read. We mean they do not *choose* to read books—or at least printed books. But imagine a time when many people could not read at all. Actually, what has happened is that as we have become more literate and have had ever more sources of information, today inundated with written materials all the time on our phones and through the Internet, we have become less inclined to take the time to read the Bible. Our problem is not literacy, but focus.

This brings me to the second preliminary point: that those who dismiss using the Bible in any sort of explanatory or careful way in church worship services have in their head a caricature of what it means to teach the Bible. I am not surprised that they have this caricature, for there are churches in the past – and perhaps also currently – who have used the Bible in church services in ways that are arcane, inaccessible, and sometimes (frankly) pompous. But just to have been exposed to *bad* models of teaching the Bible in church does not thereby mean that *good* models of teaching the Bible in church cannot exist!

And now, without further preliminaries, to the main argument. Let us look at this logically together, with the repercussions either way, and with some practical tips about how to use the Bible in church effectively too.

To begin, think what will happen if we do not use the Bible in church

For a while, people will keep on assuming the Bible is important. They will do so out of habit, tradition, and embarrassment of dismissing a book that their forebears gave their lives to protect. When someone has died for something, it takes a lot of inertia entirely to dismiss it. So there will be a season when the Bible is assumed to be the last word on religious matters, even if it is rarely consulted as such in public worship.

But what we celebrate is, in time, what we get. If we do not in our public celebrations use the Bible in any thorough way, before too long people will stop using the Bible themselves. And before too long they will stop treating the Bible as the authority on matters of life and faith. In much of the Western church, anyway, we are already in many areas close to that third step, if we have not already arrived: people, when asked about a certain matter about God or faith, will say 'I think that' or 'My opinion is' or (even more commonly) 'I feel that …' Very rarely anymore will anyone say 'The Bible says …' The reason for that lack of appeal to Scripture is because people have not had it modeled in the public worship services.

So before you remove, or continue to vacate, the Bible from public worship, think of the repercussions. Before too long you will have a generation of Christians who functionally do not treat the Bible as the authority. Why would they? After all, their public worship services have ceased treating the Bible as their functional authority. And when the Bible is no longer the functional authority for Christians, we must find other authorities.

The normal competing options are 'reason' or 'the church'. Some then will search for ancient church traditions for their authorities; others will research modern statistics, business practices, management techniques, and psychological approaches for their authorities. This is not to argue that we cannot learn anything either from reason or the church, but it is to argue that the Bible is the authority. If we do not treat it that way in church, it will not be treated that way by church people, After that, of course, will almost inevitably come – if the process is not reversed – a day when people have no biblical tools to answer false teaching. Why would they have any biblical tools to answer false teaching? They have not been reading or using the Bible!

So a church that does not use the Bible in its public worship services is risking that people who go to that church will, in time to come, in all likelihood become heretics or lose their faith. If someone has no good grasp of the Bible to be able to answer, from the Bible, fairly basic false teaching related to the Trinity, or human sexuality, or the relationship between social justice and evangelism—well, the results are predictable. Such people will, unless God intervenes and unless the Bible is taught and received, become non-Trinitarian, sexually confused, and lose their confidence in spoken personal evangelism—which is pretty much the situation you see in the contemporary church. All because churches are not teaching the Bible!

Then, think what will happen if we do use the Bible in church

Now, I do not mean use the Bible in an extremely boring way, nor use archaic language. I do not mean be extremely intellectual and impractical, nor mean preaching simply as a running commentary on the text where the goal of the sermon is to impart information about the text to the congregation. As I sometimes say, preaching is not preaching the Bible; preaching is preaching the Bible *to people*!

When I say 'use the Bible in church', I mean it in a way that is concordant with best practices, outlined in the Bible, and illustrated in contemporary churches and throughout church history. Imagine what would happen if the Bible was used in church so that the biblical message was taught, received, believed, heard, accepted, and put into practice! Would it not be the case that the people in that church would gradually become more like Christ, more loving, more engaged with the contemporary culture around them, more inclined to invite non-Christians to that church to hear from God, more able to articulate their faith themselves, more secure and not tossed around by every wind of false teaching, growing, developing and increasing more and more into the head of the church, that is Christ (Eph. 4:14-15)?

But you will say, how do we accomplish this? This is not the place for a full articulation of the use of the Bible in church, nor can this be the place for modeling and training in preaching the Bible, which is as much an art as it is a science. But here are *five practical tips* for using the Bible in church today.

#1 Use a modern translation that speaks in modern English

If the prevailing feeling is that the Bible was written a long time ago, is inaccessible and impractical, then we are not helping ourselves if the translation we use speaks in archaic language. I fully understand that 'translation wars' are a slumbering dragon in many contemporary churches, and I have no intention of waking the sleeping dragon. But whichever of the several excellent modern translations you employ, make sure it uses language that is spoken in contemporary English.

#2 Use a modern translation that is an actual translation and understand what kind of translation it is

There are a variety of good translations today, and they have different translation philosophies that influence the end result that we have in front of us. There are also 'paraphrases' that make no pretence of being a translation, but that can also aid your understanding of the Bible and appreciation of it. There is nothing wrong with paraphrases, but they should not be the main go-to of a public worship service. You want a real translation, one that is attempting to put the ancient text into modern English—not one that is giving a kind of up-to-date running commentary on the text like a paraphrase. Of course, some modern translations are more literal, some are less so. Which means that of the many good translations that are around in English today – more than in any other generation that has ever existed – make sure you know what kind of translation it is. Some require more communication work on the part of the preacher to put the text into contemporary expression; some require more communication work on the part of the preacher to explain the meaning of the text behind the smooth-sounding translated phrases. Either way, you just want to make sure you know whether you are dealing with a more literal or a less literal translation.

#3 Do not confuse exposition with exegesis

To *exegete* a passage is to explain it in its original context; a commentary is an exegesis. But preaching is far more than merely a commentary: that is only the first step of preaching. Once you have understood what the passage means, you now need to exposit it (and not merely exegete it). To *exposit* a passage is to explain it in its original context and apply it to its contemporary context. Application therefore is not a tag on to serious Bible preaching. It is inherent to the task of exposition. To exposit a passage is to expose its meaning to the people in front of you. (Preaching is not preaching the Bible; preaching is preaching the Bible to people.) Clarifying this alone would solve most of the contemporary confusion. People who are against expository preaching are often really against exegetical preaching—in the sense that they are against the kind of preaching that does not speak in contemporary terms, is irrelevant, and does not attempt to apply the passage. I am against that kind of preaching too. We must not be like the Pharisees who place burdens on people's backs and will not help them carry them. Our task is to feed the flock, not throwing impressive looking bread at any passing intellectual seagulls in our congregation.

#4 Remember the difference between a good sermon, a better sermon, and the best kinds of preaching

A good sermon is one that explains the passage, applies it faithfully, and does both in a way that is understandable, clear, and reasonably interesting. A better sermon is one that does all of that, plus does it with excellence and skill. Some people are just better preachers than other people—and people can become better preachers if they work at it. The best kind of sermons of all, however, have a touch of God about them; there is an anointing from God. Not all preachers are like this; not all sermons are like this even from the preachers who do have this anointing. We can, then, work to make sure that we do not have bad sermons. Bad sermons are those that either fail to explain the text faithfully or, if they do explain the text faithfully, fail to communicate it clearly or interestingly. The worst thing of all is to be a heretic; the next worst thing is to explain the truth but to do it boringly. The one preaches heresy; the other creates heretics. For if the truth is boring, then it will tend to encourage those who listen to such truth to look for something more interesting. Good sermons are at least clear and clearly interesting. Better sermons have something of an excellence to them. Best sermons have God's anointing. The last kind of sermon we cannot guarantee. It is up to God. We can pray and seek His favor, but it is God who moves in this way. But we can ensure that, in our churches, we have at least good sermons, and are moving towards better sermons.

#5 Do what you can to ensure that the format around the experience is not archaic

Aesthetics do matter. There is a limit to how much, perhaps, we can create a first rate 'feel' to the worship service and physical building of our particular church. But if we are looking to have the Bible used in our public worship, we do not want at the same time to indicate that we are the sort of church that is stuck in the past. We want to indicate that the Bible speaks today (and not just yesterday) by having an ambience that is not merely speaking of yesterday. There are lots of creative ways to use modern technology, style, aesthetics—not in an insecurely fashionable way that will be out-of-date before we finish doing whatever updates we are doing, but in a classy way that indicates that we are building for the kingdom of God and the glory of God, that we have a legacy, but that we are also speaking of God's Word that *is* 'living and active' (Heb. 4:12) today and tomorrow (and not just *was* living and active in the past).

A story

Jane found herself drawn to a church that only rarely, if ever, used the Bible. Of course, they had Bibles: they believed in the Bible. But when it came to the actual main meeting of the church, the Sunday morning gatherings, the Bible was conspicuous by its absence. Actually, after a while Jane hardly noticed that it wasn't there. Every now and then the pastor would make a reference to a Bible, perhaps even quote the Bible verse, and that seemed quite sufficient. Instead, the messaging of the church was far more practical. There were many more illustrations and stories, there was drama and a lot of video clips too. The Bible? Not so much.

Bit by bit, though, Jane began to realize that the lack of the Bible in the worship gathering was affecting her. A friend asked her why she believed in the Trinity, and she realized she had no biblical answer to that question. She began to make excuses for certain behaviors in her life: after all, everyone does it. And when she tried to push back against her weakening conscience, she couldn't bring up the relevant Bible verses. Jane decided she had better make a switch; she started to attend a Bible-teaching church. A year later, Jane found that she had good biblical knowledge and was able to answer her friends' questions. She also now wanted to obey Christ in every area of her life.

Questions for discussion

1. Do you think the Bible should be taught in church worship services?

2. What could you do to encourage the teaching of the Bible in your church?

3. How could you encourage those who preach the Bible?

4. If you are a preacher, what steps could you take to improve your preaching?

5. What steps could you take to improve your listening to preachers and sermons?

QUESTION 8

Does the Bible Make You Stupid?

Many people today think so. They think that because they assume that the Bible asks people to believe things that everyone knows are not true anymore. Therefore, they assume that the effect of being committed to the Bible must be to learn to live in cognitive dissonance. This is a polite way of saying that those who take the Bible seriously must be learning to live with things that they surely must know are not really true. If therefore they are not actually 'stupid' (which would be a really impolite thing to say), they are at least being forced to act as if they are. Surely bright, intelligent people must be compartmentalizing when they read the Bible and go to a biblical church: how else could a modern, educated, psychologically-normal person believe in an invisible God, a young Earth, walking on water, not to mention sexual and gender norms that are no longer considered to be 'normal'?

The way to answer this question is to take a step back and ask if the assumptions are correct and therefore if the data is accurate.

So, are the assumptions correct? That is, is it true that to believe the Bible is (as Lewis Carroll put it in *Alice Through the Looking Glass*) to learn to believe six impossible things before breakfast? If that were true, then surely it would be polite to say that to believe the Bible leads to cognitive dissonance, but perhaps too polite an understatement. If you come across people who literally believe that there are fairies at the bottom of their garden or gnomes in their basement, then you would be forgiven for thinking that they are either stupid or fooling themselves. But is the assumption correct? Is it indeed correct that to believe the Bible and take it seriously is to believe six impossible things before breakfast? Let us take some of the most common assumptions in this regard and see if they add up.

Let us consider, for instance, the much-vexed notion of *who wrote the Bible*. Is it true that to take the Bible seriously, you have to ignore all that modern historical evidence has collected regarding the multiple authors of the Bible, the process of canonicity (whereby various books in the Bible were accepted as authoritative and others rejected), and the textual manuscript evidence? Not at all. In fact, it is arguable that there is more evidence today for the reliability of the Bible then ever before. We know more about the manuscripts. We have more archaeological support and a greater appreciation for the historicity of, say, Luke. There is less reason today than ever to doubt the reliability of the Bible.

Our trouble is not evidence that undermines the reliability of the Bible, but spurious (often Internet-fueled) so-called evidence, taken out of context and without understanding, presented in soundbites, that confuses the unaware and the uneducated. You can deny the authority of the Bible for personal, intellectual, or philosophical reasons, and be living in cognitive cohesion; but to deny the Bible because of 'who wrote the Bible' being doubtful is to deny the fact that we have more evidence about the Bible today than ever before.

Or, let us consider the even more vexed questions of *science and the Bible*. This usually comes down to the view one takes about the first few chapters of Genesis and its creation account, but it is more nuanced than merely that. To take the more nuanced issue first, it is not true that to be a Bible-believing Christian means that you expect that miracles will happen at any moment and therefore the underlying foundation of scientific objectivity is undermined. In fact, the very reverse is true: the reason why we expect order in the universe, and can research into the universe with the assumption that it is explicable, is because we think that God is a God of order. One of the challenges of a more secular approach to life is that there is no underlying *reason* to *find reason* in the universe. We are constantly surprised to discover that the world is a reasonable place, and yet we constantly must deny that there is behind it all a Reasoning Mind. That truly is to live in cognitive dissonance, to find philosophical reasons to deny there is a reason for things.

But then let us take the more obvious issue of the so-called *creation vs. evolution debate*. I will no doubt get into trouble for saying it, but the task of Christian teachers is to teach, not to dissimulate to cover their back. So here goes. There is absolutely no reason why a biblical Christian cannot at the same time accept the scientific theory of evolution. Note I phrase that carefully: there are multiple reasons (theological, ethical, philosophical, moral) why a biblical Christian must reject the philosophy of evolutionary pseudo-scientism. That philosophy has lead to eugenics (the experimentation on the less well-gifted genetically that occurred before and during the Second World War) and to the killing of countless babies and, potentially, the ceasing of life to the aged when they are deemed no longer useful to society. That philosophy of evolutionary pseudo-scientism is – again I say it carefully – evil.

But the science of evolution can be logically, has been historically, and is right now currently, accepted by many biblically-minded Christians. Christians who want to argue that seven-day creation is the only way to interpret the first few chapters of Genesis will want to deny that that is the case—but the truth of the matter is, even if they are mistaken, many biblical Christians do not think that the first few chapters of Genesis run counter to Darwin's evolutionary scientific theory. My favorite example of this is the great Christian teacher Augustine. If Augustine, writing a long time before Darwin, was willing to say that Genesis chapter 1 was not to be interpreted literally (because it describes how light is created before the sun is created), then we must surely allow that there is a range of options that is legitimately present to Christian conscience. Certainly, you can also be a seven-day creationist and be a biblical Christian; I am simply saying it is not the only option.

If you want to know what I think: I'm not sure. I know that science changes its mind, so I'm unwilling to commit fully to any scientific theory or consensus today. I also know that the main point of Genesis chapter 1 is not a scientific text book. Apart from anything else, it was written by a human (probably by Moses) about events that took place before a human could literally observe them. The words are not really poetry; they are more like prophecy or apocalyptic literature—this time the revelation not about the future, but about the past.

Then let us take the assumption with regard to *sexual and gender norms*. This is a particularly complicated and sensitive issue pastorally. That is, the reality is that when we talk about human sexuality, we are talking about some of the most personal, private, intimate matters that a human being is capable of experiencing. Therefore, to discuss such things without acknowledging all the joys and the pains, the elevations and the depressions, that are inevitably associated with such intimate experiences in our world is to be naïve in the extreme. To think that we are only dealing with what people *think* when we discuss sexuality and gender, and not also with what they *feel* and experience and long for, is to misunderstand some of the most basic elements of the way humans are. In many ways, what this topic needs is not a paragraph analyzing the assumptions, but a piece of literature, of Dostoyevsky class, to pull back the layers of the onion of human experience with regard to sexuality and gender.

That said, we must be honest and admit that what the Bible says about sex is dramatically different than what our culture says about sex. There are two options: either the Bible is wrong or our culture is wrong. If it were true that in previous days the Bible's view on sex had, broadly speaking, agreed with what culture said, then we might be tempted to think that the Bible's view on sex was simply 'outdated'. But in actuality the Bible's view on sex has always run diametrically opposed to human culture's view on sex. The Greco-Roman view of sex and gender certainly included various kinds of permitted homosexuality. Even the Victorian view of sex – famed for its prudishness – is opposed to the Bible's view of sex. There the attitude was 'sweep it under the carpet,' even 'lie back and think of Britain,' when the Bible celebrates sex as a great and glorious gift. If you doubt that, try reading Song of Solomon!

The reality is that the Bible has always been out of step with culture with regard to sex. It says that sex is both a wonderful human experience, and one that is only open to a man and a woman in a committed relationship for life. No easy divorce, then. But it also says that a man or a woman who is celibate for the whole of his or her life is in no way missing out on what sex is really about—which is the consummation of our relationship with Christ, both now and forever in the divine marriage in heaven.

So to say that to accept the Bible's view of sex makes you stupid (or nasty) is really to say that human culture has always been right and the Bible has always been wrong about sex. The trouble with that is what human culture has said about sex has been quite varied: were the Victorians wrong? Were the Greeks and the Romans wrong? Were the Egyptians wrong? Were the aristocratic experimenters of the Roaring Twenties wrong? Which of these ages was wrong, and why are we now – given that what our culture says now is different from all of these – more likely to be right?

The different views on sex cancel each other out, and we are left with the Bible's view on sex down through the years. Difficult to obey, for sure. But Mount Everest is difficult to climb, which does not make it not exist. With regard to sex, the saying is truer than anywhere else that it is not that the Bible has been tried and found untrue, but that it has been tried and found difficult. True, but difficult to obey. Thank God for His grace and mercy to all us broken people, which is the real thing we need to focus on: not only the 'law' with regard to sex (as difficult to keep as that surely is) but also the gospel with regard to sex (which means that all broken sexual addicts can find healing and a fresh start to try again today).

Now let us consider the assumption with regard to *miracles*. Surely, if anything does, this proves that to accept the Bible means that you must either be stupid or living in cognitive dissonance. When you read the defenders of miracles today, it is hard to disagree that it sounds a little intellectually fallacious: people use the word 'miracle' loosely. It was a miracle that I found a parking space; it was a miracle that I was promoted at work; it was a miracle that I fell in love. No, it wasn't. Those are not miracles; they are providences. Christians believe that God 'providentially' orders the events of this world in such a way that, while suffering also comes, even that suffering is woven together for our good and His glory. But those weavings together of events are not miracles.

Miracles are rare; that is what makes them miraculous. They are rare even in the Bible. You could argue that there are few if any out-and-out miracles, after the creation itself, in the Bible until you come to the miracles that God did to rescue His people from Egypt recorded in the Book of Exodus. Then there are few if any out-and-out miracles in the Bible until you come to the ministries of Elijah and Elisha (1 Kings 17–2 Kings 13). Once again, no obvious miracles until Jesus comes as recorded in the gospels. And then there are miracles at the hands of Jesus' apostles recorded in the Acts of the Apostles. Whether or not there are miracles after the apostolic age is a matter of debate among Christians (I think there were and still are today), but whatever you think about that, even if you think there are some of these kinds of apostolic miraculous healings today, they are still rare. If they were not rare, they would not be called miracles; they would be called normal life. And then what happened that was not miraculous would be the miracle; if miracles happened all the time, it would be a true miracle when one didn't happen.

Rapidly, you get into linguistic and logical absurdity. In fact, miracles in the Bible seemed to be associated with key redemptive acts. The rescue from Egypt. The fulfillment of that Exodus rescue in God's rescue through Jesus Christ. And the witnesses to that Messianic rescue through the ministry of the apostles. The miracles of Elijah and Elisha are probably in the same category; the kingdoms of Israel had become so spiritually compromised that God mercifully sent miracles to awaken them. It is then natural enough that where there is a huge redemptive, often missionary, act occurring, the miraculous shows up. So to believe in the Bible is not to believe that miracles happen all the time. It is to believe they happen sometimes.

What is truly illogical is to deny all the evidence pointing to such miracles – say the resurrection of Jesus – on the basis of a philosophical principle. But this is the great argument of the philosopher David Hume, and his many followers still today. Miracles are, he argued, by definition the most unlikely of all possible events; indeed, they are logically impossible; therefore, however much evidence there appears to be for a miracle, it is logical to assume that there must be another explanation. Who's making the assumptions now? Surely it is – let us be polite – unwise to assume that something cannot happen and therefore, however much evidence there is for it to have happened, it still cannot by definition have happened! Those who say miracles cannot happen are really saying it because, for other philosophical reasons, they believe God does not exist. But that means they are ruling out by presumption or prejudice any evidence that they could receive that God does exist!

Finally, let us look at the assumption that the Bible makes you stupid because it asks you to *believe in an invisible God*. We all know that what is invisible does not exist. Or do we? Today there are so many things that we know exist which are invisible to the human eye that it is hard to imagine that people still think that God being invisible means He does not exist. Electricity is invisible to the human eye; I am certainly glad electricity exists. Atoms are invisible to the human eye; atoms exist. Subatomic particles are invisible to the human eye; they too, we believe, exist.

So far, we are only describing 'material' things. But what of the unquantifiable? What of love? Because we cannot 'see' love and because love is not 'material,' are we really saying that love does not exist? You might argue that love is found in the biochemical processes of your brain cells. Good luck with your love poem. What about hope? What about the big ideas? Democracy: you cannot see that, but we all know it exists. No, to rule out God because He is invisible – and therefore to assume that people who believe the Bible are stupid because to believe the Bible means to believe in an invisible being – is itself really the foolish thing. Are we saying that for a blind man nothing exists?

A story

Bill had grown up in an elite and sophisticated environment, and being preternaturally gifted himself, he made his merry way through the required elite schooling. Emerging from the hallowed, ivy-covered halls, he discovered that he did not believe much of anything anymore. Those Christians who believed in the Bible, he thought, were living in a parallel universe where unicorns and gnomes at the end of your garden also exist! Silly—usually harmless silly unless they gained any kind of political or intellectual influence. But definitely silly.

But one day, Bill came across a professor who asked him an intriguing question. On what basis was he so convinced that what he believed was true? Bill quickly protested that he didn't really believe anything – he didn't have an ideology – he was simply living with what is. 'But how', pushed back the professor, 'are you so certain that that assumption is itself correct? On what basis rests your certitude that there is no certitude?' Bill went away fuming, but he quickly realized that as much as he didn't like it, the professor had a point. There was no logical reason for using reason to reject reason. Once he had realized that, Bill began to look around for other frameworks which could make sense of his life. He even started to read the Bible. It began to make a whole lot of sense.

Questions for discussion

1. Do you know people who have 'checked their brain at the door' because they believe in the Bible?

2. Do you know people who are intelligent and sophisticated who believe in the Bible?

3. Do you know people who have 'checked their brain at the door', who reject the Bible?

4. Do you know people who are intelligent and sophisticated who reject the Bible?

5. Would it be helpful to read the Bible more to find out who is right?

QUESTION 9

Does the Bible Prevent a Tolerant Society?

The answer to this question would seem to be a self-evident 'no' to many people. The interesting part of the question, though, is that there is another fairly large group of people in the contemporary world who would think that the answer to this question is a most definite 'yes'. Wherein lies the discrepancy?

For one group of people, the Bible is a book about love, mercy and kindness. They think of the story of the Good Samaritan (Luke 10:25-37). They think of Jesus' teaching to turn the other cheek (Matt. 5:39). They think of the well-known saying, 'Do not judge' (Matt. 7:1, NIV). They think of the great summary of the Law: 'love the Lord your God with all your heart and with all your soul and with all your mind and with all your strength… love your neighbor as yourself' (Mark 12:30-31). Given all this emphasis on love, kindness, putting God and then other people before your own desires, how could anyone think that the Bible prevents a tolerant society? Surely it calls us to something far more than mere tolerance; instead to active service, love, and compassion!

But, for another group of people, the story of the Bible is far from clear on this matter of tolerance. In fact, they would say, the Bible makes it quite apparent that while, of course, it does talk about love and all the rest, there is another part to its message which is more sinister—and puts the rest of it into a wholly different perspective. That other part of the Bible's message includes things like the conquest by Israel (the Book of Joshua); the total destruction of men, women, and children at the command of God in that conquest (Josh. 6:17); Elijah, for instance, killing the prophets of Baal at his own hand (1 Kings 18:40). And even when you come to the New Testament (for these sort of people would not say that the question is merely a matter of distinguishing between a purported difference between a 'God' of the Old Testament and a 'God' of the New Testament), there is plenty of evidence of wrath. Jesus, let it be remembered, warned of hell, 'where their worm does not die and the fire is not quenched' (Mark 9:48), more than any other biblical character. Paul talked of 'handing over to Satan' those who were sinning in the Corinthian church (1 Cor. 5:5). And the book of Revelation? Well, when you read of the grapes of wrath being pressed out in the 'winepress of the wrath of God' so that the blood of those so killed rises to the level of a horse's bridle for about 184 miles around (Rev. 14:19-20), you can't help but wonder exactly how tolerant the Bible is.

And then you add in some of the history of religion, even so-called Christian religion, presumably at least to some extent influenced by this Bible, and you talk of (for sure) the Crusades, or the way the Aboriginal peoples of Australia and the Americas were treated—as complicated historically as all that is—and you can see how people begin to think that those who say that the Bible is liable to prevent a tolerant society might have a point.

What can we say in answer to this question? The following four principles are helpful.

Remember how the Bible fits together

If you interpret the Bible *flat*, as intending to present ideal models to be followed in all cases and at all times by all people, then you will fall into all sorts of egregious mistakes. People who object to this kind of answer immediately cry foul and say, 'Well, hold on now, you're just making it all a matter of interpretation, and who's to say that *your* interpretation is right?' But think with me for a moment. What would it be like if we lived in a world that interpreted all of our communications in exactly the same way? If we interpreted a Charles Dickens' novel as being the legally-mandated pattern for all behavior for all time, or a Hollywood horror movie as being an intended moral statement of how America wants people to behave, or we interpreted a piece of poetry in the same way we interpreted flight instructions for a passenger jet (or, even worse, vice versa)? We would have chaos and confusion. But people think that we should interpret all of the many different books in the Bible the same way! But, no, not at all. All the Bible *is* authoritative. But it is *not* all the same. All is written to teach us. But some of the examples we are meant to avoid; others we are meant to copy.

So then how does the Bible fit together? Christians have an easy answer to this: and this is why you want Christians to take their Bibles seriously (and you want people of other religions to ignore large parts of their faith-writings). Everything in the Bible is assessed through the lens of the person of Jesus Christ (Luke 24:27). He is the Word (John 1:1). Even more particularly: everything in the Bible is assessed through the lens of 'Greater

love has no one than this, that someone lay down his life for his friends'
(John 15:13). Any time we are interpreting something in the Bible that does
not fit with the loving death and resurrection of Jesus Christ, then we are
interpreting the Bible incorrectly.

Remember who God is and who we are

It is not true to say that the Bible teaches us that God tolerates everything.
Thankfully not. Would you want God to tolerate rape, incest, murder, or the
Holocaust? There *is* a Day of Judgment.[1] God *is* a holy God.[2] He *is* greatly to
be feared.[3] But His judgment is *His* judgment. We are not the judges. (That
does not mean we are not meant to exercise discernment; it means we are
not meant to pretend that we can decide who is going to heaven and who
is going to hell.) His judgment is eternal.[4] It is a fearsome thought, this word
'forever,' when it is applied to hell.

There are aspects of that judgment that are expressed even in the here
and now. When God expresses that judgment and His wrath now, He does
so by 'giving us over' to the consequences of our own sin (Rom. 1:18-24,
26, 28). This means not only that when we behave in a certain way, 'sin is its
own reward' and has its own consequences, but that behind that apparently
natural and logical process stands the wrath of God actively being asserted.
Nations that are immoral become depraved and weak and are more likely to
be invaded, destroyed, and suffer as a result. The same with individual people
who give in to all sinful desires and ill discipline. They are unlikely to flourish.

---

1   Romans 14:10; 2 Corinthians 5:10; Hebrews 9:27; 1 Peter 4:5.
2   1 Samuel 2:2; Isaiah 6:3; Luke 1:49; 1 Peter 1:16; Revelation 4:8.
3   Deuteronomy 6:24; Psalm 31:19; Psalm 112:1; Luke 1:50; Revelation 11:18.
4   Matthew 25:46; Mark 9:43; 2 Thessalonians 1:9; Jude 1:7.

Because God is sovereign, He sometimes uses natural forces to express these consequences, sometimes even human figures and nations. The judicial system in a country is an agency of God's wrath against wrongdoing (Rom. 13:4), a very imperfect agency in even the fairest countries, but still setting up some standard of right and wrong, however that may be evilly twisted sometimes by malicious human authorities—who themselves will come under judgment.

When you read about some of the conquests and butchery in the Old Testament, it is important to remember two things: who God is and who we are. The Israelites themselves were also on the receiving end of invasion and exile as discipline for their own idolatry. Deuteronomy 28 sets out for Israel blessings for obedience and curses for disobedience, the curses being the same judgment that Egypt and the nations they had conquered had experienced; this prophecy was fulfilled in the exile as the righteous kings and prophets at the time understood.[5] In other words, the truth of the matter is that *fairness* or *justice* is that we all go to hell. Because God is holy and because we are sinners, the right, true, fair, just consequence is eternal damnation. Unless and until we drill into our minds that we *are sinners* and that *God is holy*, we will understand precious little of what the Bible has to say (Rom. 3:10, 19).

Remember the difference between tolerance and relativism

Relativism is the doctrine that everything is relative. Of course, Einstein in his famous general theory of relativity taught us that in terms of the natural

---

5   See 2 Kings 22:13; Jeremiah 25; 2 Chronicles 36:15-16.

universe, in terms of physics, there is a theory that is now near universally accepted (with various modifications and additions related to quantum mechanics and other more recent theories) that espouses relativity. Time and space, according to Einstein, are relative to one another—and his theory has been evidenced by the minute differences we have discovered in clocks in satellite orbit around the Earth than on the Earth. But Einstein never intended for us to conclude from his general theory of relativity that *everything* is relative. For, if everything were relative, then that general theory of relativity itself would only be relatively-speaking true!

But, nonetheless, the idea that all truth is only relatively true, depending on your perspective, upbringing, and personality is now the near-universal doctrine of our age. Part of its selling point is the thinking that relativism prevents people from judging each other and therefore prevents intolerance. Which is deliciously ironic because, in actual fact, few doctrines have proved more intolerant than the doctrine that everything is relative. What it means in practice is that anyone who does not agree with that doctrine is not tolerated! And that means that on university campuses, in businesses, in politics, we are more and more seeing shaming of those who hold to contrary opinions, political correctness run amok, shutting down of legitimate forms of free speech. None of this is tolerant!

Tolerance, which is a very mild form of Christian love, depends instead upon a contrary notion. Tolerance depends upon the reality that you disagree with what someone is saying. In fact, you think that what they are saying is wrong. You don't think that what they are saying is relatively true, because then you are really agreeing with them and you have nothing to tolerate! Tolerance is saying, 'I disagree with what you are saying, but I will allow the right you have to say it.' Relativism is saying, 'What you are arguing for is only relatively true, so you and I already agree.' Relativism is, in fact, then, not only deeply intolerant, it is intrinsically intolerant. The doctrine of relativism cannot tolerate anything because, in principle, it does not think there is any idea that is wrong which it has to tolerate! And that means that when someone says something other than relativism, there is no intellectual resources for tolerating it.

Remember where tolerance came from

This is a long and complicated history, but it is important to grasp, even if only rudimentarily. The Roman Empire had a version of relativistic tolerance which only tolerated religions as long as they also worshipped the emperor. That did not play out too well for many people, including the Christians who were tortured and killed for refusing to say, 'Caesar is Lord.' Medieval Christendom spent massive amounts of its energy attempting to pick up the pieces after the decay of the Holy Roman Empire and the mounting pressure from Islamic invasions. To do so, the church aligned quite closely with various military powers and leaders to protect the church and civilization. Successful to some degree, that strategy also sullied the church by a close association with military action.

The Protestant Reformers sought to take the church back to its pristine roots, back to the Scriptures. In doing so, they aligned themselves with various kings and princes as magistrates to protect the church against the attacks of what remained of the Holy Roman Empire and the pope. Again, that strategy was successful to some extent, but created churches that were associated with nation states. Modern tolerance was birthed in a Protestant reflection on this history, by, in particular, John Locke and Roger Williams, that caused people to ask whether it was not possible to create a society where there was freedom of religious tolerance. That kind of society was increasingly practiced in England—where Huguenots and other religious minorities, including Jewish people, fled to London and America for safety.

To put it in summary form, then: tolerance is a specifically Christian, and indeed Protestant Christian, idea. At its basis is the thought that 'the truth will come out'. It was never intended to prevent the public exercise or expression of religious beliefs, nor the advocacy for Christian morality or faith in the public realm. That is not freedom of religion; that is the freedom to oppress religion. Tolerance, to be effective, relies upon specifically Christian, Protestant, commitments: namely, the power of God's Word to persuade, the prominence of faith, the importance of personal evangelism, the separation of church from state. The Bible and Christianity, of course, call us to do *far more* than merely tolerate our neighbours. We are called to love them. But the political, civil, solution of tolerance was birthed within a specifically Christian context.

The Bible, then, is actually, when rightly understood, a defender of love in social interaction and neighborly care, and tolerance within what we know as nations and states in the modern world. Jesus' famous words to 'render unto Caesar the things that are Caesar's, and to God the things that are God's' (Matt. 22:21) were, of course, spoken within a particular setting. That setting had far more in its context than merely paying of taxes, and was intended to prevent Jesus from being pinned on the horns of a dilemma by His adversaries and point out to them their responsibility to worship Him,

Jesus, as God. They had the *image* of God on their own hearts, in a similar way that the coin had the image of Caesar on it. Therefore, they were meant to give to Caesar his tax, but also give to God – specifically the God-man standing in front of them, Jesus – their love and fealty.

Jesus' statement in Matthew 22 is about far more than merely tolerance or the separation of church and state. The Bible as a whole says a lot more about how to relate to people of different faiths and philosophies than merely to tolerate them. But it is important to understand that this true idea of tolerance is a deeply Christian one and can be faithfully drawn from Christian Scriptures, like that famous statement of Jesus' to give to Caesar what is Caesar's and to God what is God's. Our fight, as Paul would say, is not against flesh and blood but against the principalities and powers of this dark world (Eph. 6:12). Again, we do not fight as the world does, but we take every thought captive and make it obedient to Christ (2 Cor. 10:4-5).

We are not, then, naïve about the power of political discourse and office holding. We support those who lead in these areas with morality, and pray and advocate for them to defend the freedom of the church to preach the gospel and practice our faith (1 Tim. 2:1-2). We want a society that is deeply influenced by Christian values because that is a society that is most likely to flourish for all and allow the gospel to spread for the eternal salvation of all those God is calling.

A story

Rebecca had not personally met Bible-believing Christians before, but she had heard about them. They were those kooks who were always trying to shove their opinions down your throats, dominate culture and politics, and generally be a party pooper about everyone else's fun. Her exposure to them had mainly been through TV and social media, but if she was honest, that was the negative impression that had built up in her mind. A nicer, middle-class version of fundamentalist extremists—still trying to take away your freedom, but now just with a smile and a bad haircut.

Then Rebecca met Jim. Jim brought her along to his Bible study. Frankly, Rebecca only agreed because Jim looked cute. But when she was there, she was surprised to discover that no one was particularly concerned about the current political campaign. There was no literature being passed around about whom to vote for. In fact, they spent some time praying for everyone who was standing for office. That didn't last very long. Most of the time they were trying to grow their 'relationship with God' or some such thing. But when politics did come up, they weren't scheming to take over America and diss on everyone else. Really, they spent most of the time talking about Jesus. Rebecca decided she wanted to find out more about Jesus.

Questions for discussion

1. Is there a particular group of people that you find it very hard to put up with?

2. How do you think the call of the Bible to love our neighbor could help?

3. Have you come across relativism's intolerance?

4. How could you advocate for the freedom of all people to express their viewpoints?

5. How could you advocate for the freedom of Christians to preach the gospel?

QUESTION 10

Is the Bible Inerrant?

For many people, this would be the first question, so it might seem odd that it is number ten in this list of most common questions that people ask about the Bible. The reason why I have put it last (but most certainly not least) is because while it is in some ways the most important, it is also so frequently misunderstood that it is better if other questions are cleared out of the way first. The truthfulness, relevance, authority, and (indeed) inspiration of Scripture are necessary components of its inerrancy, and need to be at least begun to be grasped before the inerrancy itself can be taken on board, assessed, and appropriately and truly understood.

What do we mean by 'inerrancy'?

First, the word itself tells us: it means without error. So, when we say that the Bible is inerrant, we mean that it is without error. This is a little bit different than some other – also true – claims about the Bible, namely that it is infallible or authoritative. The word 'infallible' means that something does not fail. So, while to say that the Bible is infallible is close to saying it is inerrant, it is not the same thing.

You can believe that the Bible is infallible, but not believe that it is inerrant. Sometimes people who hold to the infallibility of the Bible, but not its inerrancy, say that the Bible is true in all that it affirms. People who hold to the inerrancy of the Bible, though, go further. They would say that not only is the Bible true in all that it affirms (and not only is it the sole source of spiritual authority for matters of life and faith), but also that the Bible does not make errors. In other words, someone who holds only to the infallibility of Scripture might – though not necessarily would – say that while the story of Jonah is true in its affirmation of the importance of repentance and the global mission of God, it is not necessary to accept that it is describing a historical event. But someone who holds to the inerrancy of Scripture might argue, if we assume that Jonah is making a historical claim to fact, that the Bible's description of Jonah being swallowed by a large fish (if not a whale) needs to be believed and defended if we are to take the Bible as inerrant.

Furthermore, those who hold to the inerrancy of Scripture frequently tend to a slippery slope view of other approaches to Scripture, even sometimes the 'infallible' approach. This is because the argument is taken up to the highest level, namely the trustworthiness of God. If, it is argued, God is trustworthy, and all Christians would say He is, then His Word must be entirely trustworthy, which means it must be inerrant.

There is another view of Scripture which some people hold which could be called the 'humanistic' or 'rationalistic' view of the Bible. Those who hold to rationalistic views of the Bible think it is neither inerrant nor infallible, nor even inspired in the traditional understanding of inspiration, but merely a record of man's religious experiences over history. If someone takes this rationalistic view of Scripture, they tend then, of course, to be open to dismissing anything in it that they think is out of date. 'That was okay for Paul, but today we know better.' Some think they can thus dismiss the authority of the Bible but still affirm the essential religious experience that the Bible in their view gives witness to, and which they themselves still want to experience. What tends to happen, though, is that without an external authority, their 'religious experience' gradually becomes little more than a religion-ified version of what they want, or what culture wants, today.

What the claim to the Bible's inerrancy is not saying

Second, having outlined very briefly what inerrancy means, by comparing it with other views of Scripture, we need also to be clear about what the claim to the Bible's inerrancy is not saying. This view of inerrancy has been so frequently misunderstood and so commonly caricatured that there is little point deciding whether the Bible is inerrant until we are about what we mean by inerrancy (as we first outlined above), but also what we do *not* mean by inerrancy!

In my experience, the most frequent confusion is between inerrancy as a claim to the Bible being without error – which is about its nature and authority – and views on hermeneutics, which is the science and art of interpreting the Bible. So you will quite commonly hear some phrase like 'wooden inerrancy.' That is a confusion of terms. 'Wooden' is a pejorative term or a judgment about how someone may interpret the Bible. When you say someone is being wooden in their interpretation, you are saying that they are interpreting something with little insight or understanding related to the author's intention.

But inerrancy is not a matter of hermeneutics (how you interpret the Bible) but authority (the nature of the Bible). You can hold to the inerrancy of Scripture and have carefully responsible approach to interpreting Scripture—and many Bible teachers who hold to inerrancy do have such carefully responsible hermeneutical approaches. B.B. Warfield, who wrote defending inerrancy, is frequently accused of being a wooden literalist. But again, what a confusion in terms! To interpret the Bible *literally* means to interpret it 'as it is', but whether or not B.B. Warfield was a wooden literalist in his interpretation of the Bible has nothing to do with his view on inerrancy (actually he had a subtle approach to interpretation of Scripture). This principle level distinction between inerrancy and hermeneutics is important because otherwise people will think that if they hold to inerrancy, they must hold to regimented or unsophisticated views of certain parts of the Bible. But that is an interpretation or hermeneutic question; it is not a question about the nature of the authority of the Bible, which is what the term inerrancy is addressing.

The other part that is frequently misunderstood is the assumption that 'inerrancy' is quite a recent idea, perhaps stemming from the late nineteenth-century conflict between more modern ways of looking at the world and more traditional ways—and that inerrancy was brought out to defend the Bible in that context. In other words, the thinking is that inerrancy is not so much a description about the nature of the authority of the Bible, but a description about a historical debate that we need to move on from today. The trouble with this way of dismissing the inerrancy of the Bible is that whether or not the word 'inerrancy' is new to the nineteenth century, the concept itself is most certainly not new. That is why, at the beginning, we made sure we understood what the word means. It means, without error.

Christians have always thought the Bible has this kind of authority. This is how Augustine treats the Bible, how Chrysostom treats it. It is also how Jesus treats the Bible: 'For truly, I say to you, until heaven and earth pass away, not an iota, not a dot, will pass from the Law until all is accomplished' (Matthew 5:18). By 'law' here, Jesus means the Old Testament because right before, in verse 17, He has talked of 'the Law and the Prophets' (a summary phrase for the Old Testament Scriptures), and so by 'Law' in verse 18, He is concisely referring to that previous way of summarizing the Old Testament. Jesus said that not a little dot of an 'i' or cross of a 't' would be removed from the Bible. That's a pretty clear claim to a hardline inerrancy.

Where does this doctrine stand in the scale of lesser and greater importance for Christians?

Third, now that we understand the doctrine a little more clearly, what is its position for Christians in the scale of lesser and greater importance? Inerrancy is not of primary importance—if we understand 'primary importance' to mean that which saves you. Certainly, we are saved through hearing the Word of God. 'Faith comes from hearing, and hearing through the word of Christ' (Rom. 10:17). But the doctrine of inerrancy is not the

Word of Christ; it is a doctrine about the Word of Christ. The Bible does not teach us that we are saved by our view on inerrancy. We are saved by Jesus, His grace received through faith. The famous verse is not, 'For God so loved the world, that he gave his only Son, that whoever believes in inerrancy should be saved …' but 'For God so loved the world, that he gave his only Son, that whoever believes *in him* should not perish but have eternal life' (John 3:16).

In other words, I certainly think there are real Christians, in some cases pious, well-meaning and influential Christian leaders, who do not hold to the doctrine of inerrancy. However, that said, I do think it is a doctrine of significant importance, that it is a serious mistake to reject it, and that for Christians, churches, and Christian institutions to reject the doctrine of inerrancy is dishonoring to God, and likely – unless God graciously intervenes – to lead to a gradual downgrade of the Christian faith. Once you say there are mistakes in the Bible, it becomes logically hard to define where those mistakes are (and are not). So while infallibility is a doctrine with an honored history, my judgment is that it does not sufficiently guard the authority of Scripture in our current intellectual climate.

Does the Bible itself claim that it has no errors?

Fourth, the Bible says, 'All Scripture is God-breathed' (2 Tim. 3:16 NIV), not some Scripture is God-breathed. The Bible says 'The words of the LORD are flawless, like silver purified in a crucible, like gold refined seven times' (Ps. 12:6 NIV), not some of the words are flawless and some of them are flawed. We have already mentioned how Jesus views the Bible (Matt. 5:18). We might also mention again how He treats the Bible as all God's Word—not just the direct quotations from God, but the human authors' words recorded in the Bible too. What the Creator God said is what the human authors say in the Bible (Matt. 19:4). The New Testament is all fully God's Word, what Paul wrote, for instance, being accorded the same authority as the 'other Scriptures' (2 Pet. 3:16).

What about the so-called errors in the Bible?

Fifth, what about the so-called errors? We should distinguish what kind of errors in the Bible are meant. It is a fact that there are many manuscripts of the Bible, and that in these manuscripts there are scribal errors. But these errors are all minor, not significant for any matter of life or doctrine. And the doctrine of inerrancy does not claim that the manuscripts are without error; it claims that the original manuscript is without error.

Some people feel that this move back to the original autographs (which no one any more possesses) is a bit of a sleight of hand and not being entirely straightforward. But because the manuscripts we possess have no doctrinally significant mistake in them, because God has ordained that the transmission of the manuscripts is thoroughly reliable, to say the original autographs are inerrant means that we can – for all intents and purposes – say that the Bible in our hands is inerrant. The alternative would be to deny inerrancy of the original manuscripts, which would then undermine the authority of the Bible that we read.

With other so-called errors, due diligence requires that we find out whether the intention of the original author is to make a claim that is palpably false (in other words, are we dealing with an error of our human interpretation, not an error in the text?). With some controversial matters of interpretation of the Old Testament, we are to judge by the golden lode: what Jesus says and what the New Testament says become our guide to interpreting the Old Testament. When we come across so-called errors in the New Testament, we trust God for further light and insight, and He will give us that if we need it—as time and time again the Bible is more intellectually and rationally defensible today than ever before.

So, is the Bible inerrant? Yes.

A story

Initially, Crystal found it hard to wrap her mind around the idea of the Bible's inerrancy. She knew that there were many different translations of the Bible, and when she had compared them, they seemed to have some differences even if those differences were minor. What is more, while she understood that there was an 'original' from which these Bible translations were translated, she had heard that there were many different manuscripts. How then was it possible to think that the Bible was inerrant. She didn't want to cause any trouble, so she didn't say much. But to her it seemed much ado about nothing. Just let the Bible be the Bible was her motto.

But then a friend of hers decided to do something immoral. Crystal thought it was her responsibility to help her friend think about what she was planning to do. Her friend went to church, too, so Crystal pointed out that the Bible is against what her friend was planning to do. 'Oh, the Bible,' her friend said. 'It has so many errors.' Crystal was shocked by the way her friend had dismissed the Bible. It made her go back and think more carefully about inerrancy. To her chagrin, when she read the Bible, she realized that the Bible itself had a high claim to inerrancy. And now she rejoices in every word that it recorded.

Questions for discussion

1. Do you think the Bible has errors?

2. What does the character of God mean in terms of your approach to God's Word?

3. How would you defend the Bible against the charge that it is full of mistakes?

4. Is there any part of God's promises in the Bible that have let you down?

5. If God is faithful, and His Word reliable, how can you put more of the Bible into living practice today?

Acknowledgments

A book is a work that requires the support, counsel and input of many people. I am especially grateful for the excellent work of Willie MacKenzie and Christian Focus, for that of Colin Duriez with his skillful craft as editor, and the brilliance of agent extraordinaire Steve Laube. I am overwhelmed with gratitude for the love and friendship of my wife, Rochelle, and for the great joy that comes from doing life together as a family. Most of all my hope is that this book would receive the commendation of the Lord Jesus Christ, and my goal is that it brings Him great honor. Soli Deo Gloria.

Also available from Christian Focus …

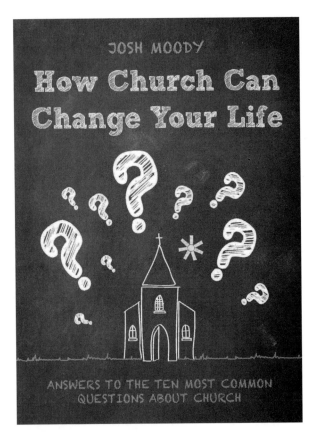

JOSH MOODY

How Church Can Change Your Life

ANSWERS TO THE TEN MOST COMMON
QUESTIONS ABOUT CHURCH

ISBN 978-1-78191-611-7

How Church Can Change Your Life
Answers to the Ten Most Common Questions about Church
JOSH MOODY

Google 'books on church', there will be no shortage of choice! Some will be helpful, others less so. So why another book on church? Josh Moody is, in fact, asking a very different question: why should I go to church at all? Filled with practical advice, this book will help you answer questions you maybe should have known the answer to and other questions you never knew to ask!

... a powerful and needed reminder of the central role the local church should play in the life of every Christian.

Albert Mohler
President, The Southern Baptist Theological Seminary,
Louisville, Kentucky

This book answers questions about the church that your friends are asking!... Read this book and be encouraged by his answers, and then pass it along to a friend who has considered church attendance to be optional.

Erwin Lutzer
Senior Pastor, Moody Church, Chicago, Illinois

This book is just brilliant!

Steve Levy
Pastor, Mount Pleasant Baptist Church, Swansea, Wales

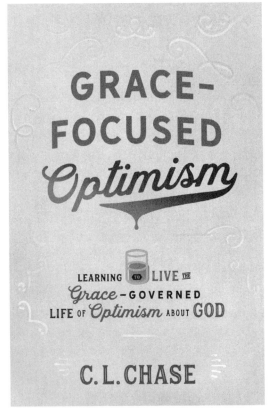

GRACE-FOCUSED
Optimism

LEARNING TO LIVE THE
Grace - GOVERNED
LIFE OF *Optimism* ABOUT GOD

C. L. CHASE

ISBN 978-1-5271-0042-8

Grace-Focused Optimism
Learning to Live the Grace-Governed Life of Optimism About God
C. L. CHASE

Grace is not merely a word on a page. It is a truth which has power in our lives—it is God's invincible determination, through Jesus, to get glory from us by being good to us every day, all day long. Understanding grace leads to an optimism, rooted and grounded in our good and unchangeable God. C. L. Chase opens up the biblical truths associated with grace and promised to every believer, helping to show the adventure of a grace-governed life.

Dr. Charley L. Chase will not let you forget that God Almighty loves you and is on your side. He gently reminds us, through his Grace Focused Optimism conferences, gfoministries.com website, and, above all, his book, that you can't help being a joyful, blessed Christian if you focus on God's grace. His book is a treasure and resource that will lift your heart. I highly recommend it!

John Carenen
author, *Signs of Struggle* and *A Far Gone Night*

TRUTHFORLIFE®

THE BIBLE-TEACHING MINISTRY OF **ALISTAIR BEGG**

The mission of Truth For Life is to teach the Bible with clarity and relevance so that unbelievers will be converted, believers will be established, and local churches will be strengthened.

Daily Program

Each day, Truth For Life distributes the Bible teaching of Alistair Begg across the U.S. and in several locations outside of the U.S. on over 1,800 radio outlets. To find a radio station near you, visit **truthforlife.org/stationfinder**.

Free Teaching

The daily program, and Truth For Life's entire teaching archive of over 2,000 Bible-teaching messages, can be accessed for free online and through Truth For Life's full-feature mobile app. Download the free mobile app at **truthforlife.org/app** and listen free online at **truthforlife.org**.

At-Cost Resources

Books and full-length teaching from Alistair Begg on CD, DVD, and MP3CD are available for purchase at cost, with no mark up. Visit **truthforlife.org/store**.

Where to Begin?

If you're new to Truth For Life and would like to know where to begin listening and learning, find starting point suggestions at **truthforlife.org/firststep**. For a full list of ways to connect with Truth For Life, visit **truthforlife.org/subscribe**.

Contact Truth For Life

P.O. Box 398000 Cleveland, Ohio 44139
phone 1 (888) 588-7884   **email** letters@truthforlife.org
 /truthforlife   @truthforlife   truthforlife.org

Christian Focus Publications

Our mission statement –

STAYING FAITHFUL

In dependence upon God we seek to impact the world through literature faithful to His infallible Word, the Bible. Our aim is to ensure that the Lord Jesus Christ is presented as the only hope to obtain forgiveness of sin, live a useful life and look forward to heaven with Him.

Our books are published in four imprints:

CHRISTIAN FOCUS

Popular works including biographies, commentaries, basic doctrine and Christian living.

CHRISTIAN HERITAGE

Books representing some of the best material from the rich heritage of the church.

MENTOR

Books written at a level suitable for Bible College and seminary students, pastors, and other serious readers. The imprint includes commentaries, doctrinal studies, examination of current issues and church history.

CF4•K

Children's books for quality Bible teaching and for all age groups: Sunday school curriculum, puzzle and activity books; personal and family devotional titles, biographies and inspirational stories – because you are never too young to know Jesus!

Christian Focus Publications Ltd,
Geanies House, Fearn, Ross-shire,
IV20 1TW, Scotland, United Kingdom.
www.christianfocus.com
blog.christianfocus.com